THE BUBBLY BLACK GIRL SHEDS HER CHAMELEON SKIN

BOOK, MUSIC AND LYRICS BY
KIRSTEN CHILDS

DRAMATISTS
PLAY SERVICE
INC.

THE BUBBLY BLACK GIRL SHEDS HER CHAMELEON SKIN
Copyright © 2003, Kirsten Childs

All Rights Reserved

THE BUBBLY BLACK GIRL SHEDS HER CHAMELEON SKIN is fully protected under the copyright laws of the United States of America, and of all countries covered by the International Copyright Union (including the Dominion of Canada and the rest of the British Commonwealth), and of all countries covered by the Pan-American Copyright Convention, the Universal Copyright Convention, the Berne Convention, and of all countries with which the United States has reciprocal copyright relations. No part of this publication may be reproduced in any form by any means (electronic, mechanical, photocopying, recording, or otherwise), or stored in any retrieval system in any way (electronic or mechanical) without written permission of the publisher.

The English language stock and amateur stage performance rights in the United States, its territories, possessions and Canada for THE BUBBLY BLACK GIRL SHEDS HER CHAMELEON SKIN are controlled exclusively by Dramatists Play Service, 440 Park Avenue South, New York, NY 10016. **No professional or nonprofessional performance of the Play may be given without obtaining in advance the written permission of Dramatists Play Service and paying the requisite fee.**

All other rights, including without limitation motion picture, recitation, lecturing, public reading, radio broadcasting, television, video or sound recording, and the rights of translation into foreign languages are strictly reserved.

Inquiries concerning all other rights should be addressed to WME Entertainment, 11 Madison Avenue, New York, NY 10010. Attn: Susan Weaving.

NOTE ON BILLING

Anyone receiving permission to produce THE BUBBLY BLACK GIRL SHEDS HER CHAMELEON SKIN is required to give credit to the Author as sole and exclusive Author of the Play on the title page of all programs distributed in connection with performances of the Play and in all instances in which the title of the Play appears, including printed or digital materials for advertising, publicizing or otherwise exploiting the Play and/or a production thereof. The name of the Author must appear on a separate line, in which no other name appears, immediately beneath the title and in size and prominence of type equal to 50% of the size of the largest, most prominent letter used for the title of the Play. No person, firm or entity may receive credit larger or more prominent than that accorded the Author. The following acknowledgment must appear on the title page of all programs distributed in connection with performances of the Play:

THE BUBBLY BLACK GIRL SHEDS HER CHAMELEON SKIN
was first presented in New York City by Dixon Place with funds
from the Joyce Mertz-Gilmore Foundation.

Partially developed during the 1998 National Music
Theater Conference at the O'Neill Theater Center.

Developed in part at the National Alliance for Musical Theater,
Helen Sneed, Executive and Artistic Director,
and also at Musical Theater Works.

Playwrights Horizons, New York City, in association with
Wind Dancer Theatre, produced the World Premiere in 1999–2000.

In addition, the following acknowledgment must appear in all programs distributed in connection with performances of the Play:

> The Gold Medal jingle is used with the permission of General Mills, Inc.

SPECIAL NOTE ON SONGS/RECORDINGS

Dramatists Play Service neither holds the rights to nor grants permission to use any songs or recordings mentioned in the Play. Permission for performances of copyrighted songs, arrangements or recordings mentioned in this Play is not included in our license agreement. The permission of the copyright owner(s) must be obtained for any such use. For any songs and/or recordings mentioned in the Play, other songs, arrangements, or recordings may be substituted provided permission from the copyright owner(s) of such songs, arrangements or recordings is obtained; or songs, arrangements or recordings in the public domain may be substituted.

AUTHOR'S NOTE

With regard to the music: In the immortal words of that great American composer/musician James Brown, "Make it funky." Thank you.

THE BUBBLY BLACK GIRL SHEDS HER CHAMELEON SKIN was originally produced by Playwrights Horizons (Tim Sanford, Artistic Director; Leslie Marcus, Managing Director; William Russo, General Manager) in association with Wind Dancer Theatre (Pamela Ferrell McCarthy, Associate Producer) in New York City, opening on June 20, 2000. It was directed by Wilfredo Medina; the set design was by David Gallo; the lighting design was by Michael Lincoln; the sound design was by Jon Weston; the musical director was Fred Carl; the orchestrations were by Joe Baker; the costume design was by David C. Woolard; the choreography was by A.C. Ciulla; and the production stage manager was Alexis Shorter. The cast was as follows:

MISS PAIN, HARRIET TUBMAN,
SECRETARY, TALLULAH, GRANNY .... Cheryl Alexander
EMILY, NILDA, SANDRA .... Natalie Venetia Belcon
LARRY, KEITH .... Duane Boutté
GREGORY .... Darius de Haas
CHITTY CHATTY PAL 1, SECRETARY,
BALLET TEACHER, SOPHIA .... Angel Desai
JAZZ TEACHER, DANCE CAPTAIN, LUCAS .... Jerry Dixon
PRINCE, COSMIC, POLICEMAN,
DIRECTOR BOB .... Jonathan Dokuchitz
CHITTY CHATTY PAL 2, SECRETARY,
MODERN DANCE TEACHER, SCARLETT .... Felicia Finley
DADDY, POLICEMAN .... Robert Jason Jackson
VIVECA .... LaChanze
MOMMY, YOLANDA .... Debra M. Walton

MUSICIANS

Fred Carl — Conductor/Flute
Randall Eng — Assistant Conductor/Keyboard 1
John DiPinto — Keyboard 2
Dave Richards — Bass
Joe Mowatt — Percussion

CHARACTERS

VIVECA
MOMMY
DADDY
GRANNY
BALLET TEACHER
CHITTY CHATTY PAL 1
CHITTY CHATTY PAL 2
COSMIC
DANCE CAPTAIN
DIRECTOR BOB
EMILY
GREGORY
HARRIET TUBMAN
JAZZ TEACHER
KEITH
LARRY
LUCAS
MISS PAIN
MODERN DANCE TEACHER
NILDA
POLICEMAN
PRINCE
SANDRA
SCARLETT
SECRETARY
SOPHIA
TALLULAH
YOLANDA

SETTING

From the early 1960s in L.A.
to the mid-1990s in New York.

THE BUBBLY BLACK GIRL SHEDS HER CHAMELEON SKIN

WELCOME TO MY L.A.

Darkness. Lights up on Viveca Stanton, an energetic little girl, waving happily to the world.

CHORUS.
THERE WAS A GIRL …
SHE WAS A BUBBLY BLACK GIRL …
A BUBBLY, BUBBLY BLACK GIRL
FROM CALIFORNIA …
OOH … OOH … OOH …

VIVECA. Hello, everybody! My name is Viveca Stanton, but you can call me Bubbly! Have a nice day!

VIVECA.
A CALM BREEZE ACROSS THE PALM TREES IS LIKE A
BALM EASING MY SOUL — THE WHOLE CITY OF ANGELS FEELS LIKE
HEAVEN — MY LUCKY SEVEN ON A ROLL!
THE SUN IS HOT — IT'S SHINING THROUGH THE VALLEY
I'M WALKING HOME THROUGH THE ALLEY THE AFTER-SCHOOL WAY
I'M DANCING DOWN THE STREET
I'M BOUNCING ON MY FEET THE COOL WAY

NEIGHBOR 1. Little Viveca Stanton!

NEIGHBOR 2. Her friends call her Bubbly!

GREGORY ROBINSON. She's got a twinkle in her eye, a bounce in her step, and a "have a nice day" smile!

NEIGHBOR 3. She's very, very bright —

NEIGHBOR 4. — has both parents in the home —

NEIGHBOR 5. — and not a welfare check in sight!

NEIGHBORS, GREGORY, DADDY and MOMMY. *(All smiling approvingly.)* She's one of the good ones!

VIVECA.
THE GRASS IS HIGH — IT'S CRACKING THROUGH THE SIDEWALK
BLACK BOYS ARE DOING THE STRIDEWALK TRYING TO IMPRESS ME

BOYS. *(Striding coolly by her, on their way to the hamburger joint.)* Hey Bubbly, what

you say!
VIVECA.
I WAVE AND SMILE AS THEY ADDRESS ME
(She joins them at the hamburger joint; more kids show up.)
PAST THE FAST FOOD PLACE, THE FAST CARS RACE
DOWN THE FREEWAY, DOWN THE FREEWAY
T-BIRD, MUSTANG, CADILLAC AND STINGRAY CHEVROLET
ALL ZOOMING THROUGH L.A.!
VIVECA and CHORUS.
SOME OUT-OF-TOWNERS CAN BE PUT-DOWNERS
(Imitating someone haughty.)
"L.A.'S A WASTELAND, A HAVE-NO-TASTE LAND!"
(As themselves.)
THE REAL L.A., THEY KNOW NOTHING OF IT, BUT HEY, I LOVE IT!
IT MAKES ME STRIDE! IT MAKES ME HAVE PRIDE!
IT GIVES ME L.A. COOL! I GET IT AFTER SCHOOL!
FAIRFAX, PICO, CRENSHAW, SLAUSON, WASHINGTON, JEFFERSON
ALL AROUND MY STOMPING GROUND!
(Boys do a "striding" dance; girls cheer them on and join in, ad-libbing things like, "Go Gregory!" "Go, Bubbly!" "Stride!" etc.)
LET YOUR FOOT SLIDE DOWN TO THE SEASIDE!
DON'T NEED NO SWIMMING POOL TO KEEP YOUR L.A. COOL
CATCH A MOVIE AT THE BALDWIN
GET A LITTLE HOLLYWOOD IN THE NEIGHBORHOOD!
VIVECA.
AND WE'VE GOT MALIBU, THE TAR PITS TOO
PLAYA DEL REY, HERE IN L.A.!
VIVECA and CHORUS.
HAVE A NICE DAY, HAVE A NICE DAY, HAVE A NICE DAY!
WELCOME TO MY L.A.!
(End of song. Everyone exits except for Viveca and Gregory Robinson.)
VIVECA. Thanks for walking me home, Gregory.
GREGORY. Hey, I'm spose to walk you home and protect you, Bubbly, 'cause I'm the man! *(Watching her pirouette and sashay around.)* Whatcha doin'?
VIVECA. I'm dancing around in my underwear, like Lola, in that movie, *Damn Yankees!*
GREGORY. Oooh, you better stop that! It's not nice for little girls to swear and dance around in their underwear! And if you keep on doin' it, I'm not gonna marry you when we grow up.
VIVECA. *(Discordant chord; she steps into an "inner thoughts" spotlight.)* Marry me! Oh no … next he'll be expecting me to hold his hand at recess — and then I'll have

to slow dance with him at parties — and get a crick in my neck from keeping my pressed hair away from his sweaty old cheek — and then he'll start bossing me around, and I'll never become — *(Starry-eyed, as dancing music rises.)* the greatest dancing star in the world! *(The music is now discordant.)* And I'll be miserable for the rest of my life — no way, Jose! That'll never, ever happen to me! *(Reflecting.)* … But he was nice enough to walk me home. So, I guess I'd better let him down easy … *(Stepping back into the scene with Gregory.)* Me? Marry you? *(Slapping her thigh; doubling over with laughter.)* Ah ha ha ha ha ha ha! Ah ha ha ha ha ha ha! Ah ha ha —
GREGORY. *(Sweet as pie.)* Hey, Bubbly, guess what? They killed some little girls in church yesterday.
VIVECA. They did not.
GREGORY. Uh-huh. Four little colored girls in Alabama. They trapped them down in the basement and threw a bomb in there, and blew 'em to pieces. And one of 'em looked just like you, I saw her picture in the paper, and boy, was she uglee! And she looked even uglier after they blew her up!
VIVECA. You shut up!
GREGORY. She went just like this — *(Folding his hands in prayer, he sings:)* JESUS LOVES ME, THIS I KNOW
— Boom! Guess Jesus didn't love her that much — ah ha ha ha ha ha ha!
VIVECA. You shut up, Gregory!
GREGORY. *(Running off, laughing.)* Ah ha ha ha ha ha ha! See you tomorrow — you hope! Ah ha ha ha ha ha ha!
VIVECA. You're a lie and a grunt, Gregory Robinson! *(She goes inside her house, finds the newspaper, and goes to her bedroom to read the paper. Very worried, Viveca picks up the Chitty Chatty doll on her pillow; studies the bombed girls' pictures.)* … Addie Mae Collins … Denise McNair … Carole Robertson … Cynthia Wesley — which one of these girls looks like me, Chitty Chatty?
CHITTY CHATTY. *(As Viveca pulls the ring that makes Chitty Chatty talk.)* I really love you!

SWEET CHITTY CHATTY

VIVECA.
SWEET CHITTY CHATTY, SWEET CHITTY CHATTY
SUCH A CHEERY, CHATTERING DOLL!
TUG ON HER TELLTALE STRING
SWEET, SWEET CHITTY CHATTY STARTS CHITTY-CHATTING!

VIVECA.	**CHATTY PAL 1.**
SWEET CHITTY CHATTY, MY LITTLE	SWEET CHITTY CHATTY, SWEET CHITTY CHATTY
FRECKLE FACE BUTTON NOSE	SUCH A CHEERY, CHATTERING DOLL!

PERKY SMILING BLUE EYE BLOND
SWEET CHITTY CHATTY
VIVECA.
I REALLY LOVE YOU
VIVECA and CHATTY PAL 2.
SWEET CHITTY CHATTY, 'CAUSE
THOUGH MY SKIN IS BROWN
YOU DON'T FROWN — SMILE AND
SAY, "PLEASE PICK ME UP"
YOU MAKE ME HAPPY
CHITTY CHATTY, SAVE ME
TELL ME WHY THE WORLD'S SO CRAZY
TELL ME WHY IT HAS TO BE
MEN THROW BOMBS AT KIDS LIKE ME
IN CHURCHES IN BIRMINGHAM?
VIVECA.
I'M PRAYIN' TO YOU
VIVECA and CHATTY PAL 2.
SWEET CHITTY CHATTY
I FEEL YOUR DIMPLED GRIN
ON MY CHIN WHEN I KISS YOUR
PLASTIC CHEEK
SWEET CHITTY CHATTY
VIVECA.
HEY, CROSS YOUR FINGERS
VIVECA and CHATTY PAL 2.
SWEET CHITTY CHATTY —
IF THEY DON'T BLOW ME UP
I'LL GROW UP — HOPE I TURN OUT
JUST LIKE YOU
SWEET CHITTY CHATTY
SWEET CHITTY CHATTY
SWEET CHITTY CHATTY…

TUG ON HER TELLTALE STRING — SWEET, SWEET
CHITTY CHATTY STARTS CHITTY-CHATTING!

CHATTY PAL 1.
SWEET CHITTY CHATTY, SWEET CHITTY CHATTY
SUCH A CHEERY, CHATTERING DOLL!
TUG ON HER TELLTALE STRING — SWEET, SWEET
CHITTY CHATTY STARTS CHITTY-CHATTING!
WATCH OUT FOR THE BOMB, NOW!
WATCH OUT FOR THE BOMB, NOW!
BOMB, BOMB, BOMB, BOMB!
BOMB, BOMB, BOMB, BOMB!
WATCH OUT FOR THE BOMB, NOW —
BOOM!

CHATTY PAL 1.
SWEET CHITTY CHATTY, SWEET CHITTY CHATTY
SUCH A CHEERY, CHATTERING DOLL!
TUG ON HER TELLTALE STRING — SWEET, SWEET
CHITTY CHATTY STARTS CHITTY-CHATTING!

CHATTY PAL 1.
SWEET CHITTY CHATTY, SWEET CHITTY CHATTY
SUCH A CHEERY, CHATTERING DOLL!
TUG ON HER TELLTALE STRING —
SWEET, SWEET CHITTY CHATTY STARTS CHITTY-CHATTING!
SWEET, SWEET CHITTY CHATTY STARTS CHITTY-CHATTING!
SWEET, SWEET CHITTY CHATTY STARTS CHITTY-CHATTING!

(End of song.)
MOMMY. *(Offstage.)* Viveca, what are you doing in there?
VIVECA. *(Throwing down Chitty Chatty; grabbing her black doll, yelling out:)* I'm reading my pictorial history of the American Negro to my Negro baby doll, Mommy!
MOMMY. That's very nice, but you should be starting your homework.
VIVECA. Okay! *(She stares at her black doll, throws it down, says:)* Boom! *(Conspiratorially, to Chitty Chatty as she retrieves her:)* She's not like us, huh, Chitty Chatty? Hey — want to know a secret? But you have to keep it really quiet. Okay?

Okay! Well, Chitty Chatty, I've decided I'm gonna be— *(Suddenly cautious; whispering:)* Wait a minute — *(She goes to the door, peeps down the hallway, comes back inside her room, picks up Negro baby doll, shoves her under the bed.)* I've decided I'm gonna be white! Just like you, Chitty Chatty. Uh-huh. And one day a prince is gonna come and rescue me from this evil, awful spell that a wicked witch has cast upon me. My prince shall kiss me, and my kinky, kinky hair shall straighten and grow down, down, down to my behind. My eyes shall turn as blue as a robin's egg, my skin as white as the virgin snow, and my prince shall say to me:

PRINCE. *(Entering from out of a fairy tale book.)* Ah, Viveca, Viveca, Viveca! How glad I am that you were so clever as to hide inside the little white girl chamber of your mind while you waited so, so patiently for me! But wait no longer, Viveca, for I am here and ready to carry you off in my brawny, brawny arms!

VIVECA. Just like Richard Chamberlain carried off Yvette Mimieux in the "Tyger, Tyger" episode of *Dr. Kildare*, except I shan't be dead, my sweet prince, because I did not fall off my surfboard while I was having a grand mal epileptic seizure when I went out surfing after the doctor told me not to, like dumb old Yvette!

VIVECA and PRINCE. *(As they hear approaching parental footsteps:)* Uh-oh! Daddy's home! Farewell! *(The prince dashes away; Viveca chucks Chitty Chatty underneath the bed, retrieves her black doll, a huge black book, reading just as Daddy arrives.)*

VIVECA. … and then Harriet Tubman pointed the gun at the slave's head and said, "You gonna be free or die!"

DADDY. Viveca, didn't your mother tell you to start doing your homework about an hour ago?

VIVECA. *(Pointing to the church bombing article in the newspaper.)* Daddy, is that going to happen to me?

DADDY. No, it's not going to happen, Vivvie. Remember the magic thing I told you to say when you start to get scared?

DADDY and VIVECA. "Smile, smile, things are not as bad as they seem."

VIVECA. I tried that, Daddy, it didn't work.

SMILE, SMILE

DADDY. Try again, Vivvie. Come on, don't let me down …
A HAPPY SMILE ON A HAPPY FACE
IS A GIFT FROM GOD TO LIFT UP THE HUMAN RACE
SO SMILE, SMILE, LET YOUR HEART BE FREE —
DOESN'T COST A THING AND IT'S BEAUTIFUL TO SEE
DADDY and DADDIES 2, 3, 4 and 5. *(As lights come up on four other fathers, singing along with Daddy.)*
I KNOW IT'S ROUGH, WHEN YOU'RE FEELING SAD

WHEN THE BEST YOU'VE GOT IS THE WORST YOU'VE EVER HAD
BUT SMILE, SMILE — WON'T YOU CARE TO TRY?
MAY NOT SEEM LIKE MUCH, BUT SOMETIMES IT GETS YOU BY
DADDY. *(Waltzing with Viveca.)*
VIVVIE, SMILE FOR ME
DON'T EVER LET THEM KNOW YOU FEEL THE PAIN
THEIR LOSS — YOUR GAIN
DON'T THINK THAT IT'S WEAK TO TURN YOUR CHEEK
OUTCLASS THEM WITH STYLE — GO THE EXTRA MILE
DADDY and DADDIES 2, 3, 4 and 5.
ON THE SEARCH FOR FAITH, IN THE QUEST FOR FAME
IN THE NAME OF LOVE, OR A MORE BELOVED NAME …
DADDY 2.
DENISE —
DADDY 3.
CAROLE —
DADDY 4.
ADDIE MAE —
DADDY 5.
CYNTHIA —
DADDY.
VIVECA —
DADDY and DADDIES 2, 3, 4 and 5.
(As lights go down on the other four fathers.)
SMILE, SMILE JUST A LITTLE WHILE
THERE'S A RAY OF HOPE IN THE SUNLIGHT OF YOUR SMILE
DADDY.
SMILE, SMILE JUST A LITTLE WHILE — WON'T YOU MAKE MY DAY?
WON'T YOU LET ME SEE YOU SMILE?
(End of song.) Remember, Vivvie, I'm counting on my little girl to show her best face to the world.
VIVECA. I won't let you down, Daddy! *(She picks up the paper, glances at it; forces a smile as she hands it to Daddy and exits. Mommy enters; Daddy shows her the paper.)*
DADDY. Why was this in her room?!
MOMMY. I didn't put it in there, but maybe it's good she read it. She's always in there, dancing with that white doll, pretending she's in a fairy tale where white is good and black is bad. Maybe she needs to see that sometimes monsters can be white.
DADDY. She's dancing in her room because she's practicing for her ballet tryouts. What harm can there be for my little girl to have her dreams?
MOMMY. She's my little girl, too, and those dreams she has are going to hurt her some day!

DADDY. Keep your voice down!
MOMMY. And you keep sugarcoating things for her, and watch what happens!
MISS PAIN. *(Lights up on Viveca, Gregory, his little sister Yolanda and Emily in ballet class. Miss Pain, the austere teacher, raps on her cane.)* The day for the Sleeping Beauty dance recital tryouts has arrived, children! As we go through our ballet routine today, I'll be deciding what parts you will play, so put your best foot forward! *(To Gregory, who sticks his foot out in a silly way.)* Gregory Robinson, act your age and not your color! Andiamo!

I AM IN DANCE CLASS

VIVECA.
I AM IN DANCE CLASS — I LOVE TO BE HERE
DOING LOTS OF MOVEMENT
I'M GETTING GOOD NOW — MISS PAIN, MY TEACHER
SAYS I SHOW IMPROVEMENT
AND TODAY'S THE DAY THAT I HOPE SHE'LL SAY I'LL PLAY
SLEEPING BEAUTY — I'VE PRACTICED FOR IT REALLY, REALLY HARD
AND IF I DON'T MESS IT UP, MAYBE I WILL BE THE PRINCESS!
YOLANDA. *(Hopelessly bad; distracted and annoyed.)*
I AM IN DANCE CLASS, AND THE BEATLES ARE IN LIVERPOOL
WITHOUT ME, AND I'M MISSING ALL MY CHANCES
PAUL McCARTNEY'S STILL SINGLE
BUT JANE ASHER'S GONNA SNAG HIM WHILE I'M STUCK HERE
TRYING TO LEARN THESE STUPID DANCES
OH I WISH I COULD FLEE TO MY HUSBAND-TO-BE
PAUL McCARTNEY!
INSTEAD I'M STUCK IN STINKY DANCE CLASS
DANCE CLASS — P.U.! I HATE IT!
EMILY. *(Naturally gifted, sneaking wistful glances at Gregory.)*
I AM IN DANCE CLASS — AND IT'S WONDERFUL 'CAUSE I'M HERE
NEAR A CERTAIN PERSON — I AM SO HAPPY
'CAUSE HE SPENDS A LOT OF TIME HERE
WHEN WE START REHEARSIN'
GREG'RY ROBINSON'S PLAYING THE PRINCE
AND THOUGH I WON'T BE THE PRINCESS
HE'S TALL AND SKINNY AND FUNNY AND CUTE
AND HE'S WHY I LOVE TO BE IN DANCE CLASS!
MISS PAIN.
EMILY, PLEASE BRING UP YOUR ARM ONE MORE INCH
GREGORY, YOU DON'T HAVE THE SENSE OF A CHINCH!

VIVECA, THAT'S BETTER — YOLANDA, YOU'RE DOING JUST FINE! ANDIAMO!
GREGORY. *(Bored out of his mind, as he indicates Yolanda.)*
I AM IN THIS DANCE CLASS 'CAUSE I HAVE TO BABYSIT HER
SHE'S MY STUPID LITTLE SISTER, AND I'D LIKE TO MAYBE HIT HER
BUT MY DAD SAID HE WILL BUY ME A BIKE IF I DO THIS
I THINK I'M GONNA GET A STINGRAY — RIDE WITH NO HANDS!
Yeah!
I'LL POP SOME WHEELIES!
VIVECA. *(To Emily; indicating Yolanda and herself.)*
I HATE TO SAY THIS
BUT YOU ARE BETTER THAN THE TWO OF US
EMILY.
WELL, IT DOESN'T MATTER IF I'M BETTER, 'CAUSE THE GIRL WHO
IS THE LIGHTEST WILL BE CHOSEN FROM THE FEW OF US
VIVECA.
NO, MY MOMMY SAYS BLACK IS BEAUTIFUL
COLOR MAKES NO DIFFERENCE
IF BLACK IS BEAUTIFUL, PLUS YOU'RE THE BEST
YOU CAN FORGET ALL THE REST, LITTLE PEST
YOU'LL BE THE PRINCESS!
EMILY.
YEAH, THEY ALL SAY THAT — WHAT THEY REALLY MEAN IS
"SAY IT LOUD, I'M BLACK, BUT PROUD
I'M NOT THE BLACKEST IN THE CROWD!"
VIVECA.
THAT IS PATHETIC!
EMILY.
YOU'RE PATHETIC IF YOU'RE FIGURIN' THAT DARKER SKIN
WILL EVER HELP YOU WIN — NOW YOU CAN BE THE COURT JESTER
THE SCULLERY MAID, OR THE MONSTER
YOLANDA. *(Overhearing from the "court jester" part; piping in eagerly.)*
I'D LIKE TO BE THE FIRE-BREATHING DRAGON
WHO SLAYS THE PRINCE! OH YEAH!
VIVECA.
EMILY, YOU'RE GONNA BE PICKED — IT'S A CINCH!
EMILY.
VIVECA, YOU DON'T HAVE THE SENSE OF A CHINCH!
MISS PAIN.
GREGORY, THAT'S BETTER — YOLANDA, YOU'RE DOING JUST FINE!
ANDIAMO!

VIVECA.	YOLANDA.	EMILY.	GREGORY.
I am in dance class	I am in dance class	I am in dance class	I am in this dance class
I love to be here	And the Beatles are in	and it's wonderful, 'cause	'cause I have to babysit her
Doing lots of movement	Liverpool without me	I'm here with a certain	She's my stupid little sister
I'm getting good now	And I'm missing all my	person — I am so happy	and I'd like to
Miss Pain, my teacher	chances — Paul McCartney's	'cause he spends a lot of	maybe hit her
Says I show improvement	still single but Jane Asher's	time here when we start	but my dad said he will
And today's the day	gonna snag him while I'm	rehearsin' — Greg'ry	buy me a bike
that I hope she'll say	stuck here trying to learn	Robinson's playing the	if I do this —
I'll play	these stupid dances — oh I	prince, and though I won't	I think I'm gonna get a
Sleeping Beauty	wish I could flee to my	be the princess	Stingray!
I've practiced for it	husband-to-be, Paul	he's tall and	Ride with
really, really hard	McCartney — instead I'm	skinny and	no hands!
And if I don't	stuck in stinky dance class!	funny and cute	Yeah!
mess it up, maybe	Dance class — P.U.!	And that's why I love	I'll pop some
I will be the best in —	I hate this —	to be near him in —	wheelies in this —

VIVECA, GREGORY, EMILY and YOLANDA.
DANCE CLASS!
(End of song.)

MISS PAIN. Very good, children. Now, for the recital, Gregory shall play the prince, Yolanda shall play Sleeping Beauty —

GREGORY. No bicycle is worth that much!

MISS PAIN. *(Catching Gregory by the arm as he starts to bolt.)* Emily shall play the court jester, and Viveca shall be the dancing bramble bush. Let's go look at the costumes to see if they fit.

EMILY. *(To Viveca as Miss Pain, Gregory and Yolanda exit:)* Don't take it so hard, Viveca. That's just the way it is. Gregory looks like the prince, and Yolanda looks like the princess.

DADDY. *(Entering, as Emily exits and Viveca returns to her bedroom.)* So? How'd it go?

VIVECA. *(Bitterly.)* Miss Pain picked Yolanda for the princess, but it's only because Yolanda is — *(Mommy enters; Viveca notices Mommy's skin color, then her own. Viveca looks down, mumbling.)* Never mind, I don't want to go to dance class any more, anyway. I've got too much schoolwork. *(Daddy exits; Viveca picks up Chitty Chatty, turning away from Mommy's attempt to comfort her. Mommy exits. Viveca feels bad, blurts out:)* Mommy… *(It's too late; Mommy's gone. Hugging Chitty Chatty.)* Smile, smile, things are not as bad as they seem. *(Cheered by a new thought, dancing with Chitty Chatty.)* Because I can still be the greatest dancing star — when I go to junior high school! They'll have dance classes over there! *(Sudden, anxious thought.)* They'll have white kids over there, too. Do you think they'll be nice, Chitty Chatty? Do you think they'll like me? *(Lights out, then lights up on a sign saying, "Louis Pasteur Junior High School Gymnasium." Viveca enters the gym. Girls of all ethnicities are exercising in gym shorts. They start to dance.)*

THE SKATE

VIVECA.
JUNIOR HIGH SCHOOL CALLED LOUIS PASTEUR
LITTLE BLACK GIRL KINDA INSECURE
OH BUT ON THURSDAYS AT TWO, I SURE FEEL GREAT
BECAUSE IN THE GIRL'S GYM, YOU GET TO DO THE SKATE!
WE WEAR THOSE WHITE TENNIS SHOES THAT YOU
WEAR FOR SPORTS, AND THEN THOSE WHITE SNAP SHIRTS
AND THOSE LITTLE GREEN SHORTS, NOW YOU CAN
BLEACH IT, YOU CAN RAT IT, YOU CAN PRESS YOUR HAIR
BUT AT TWO IN THE GYM, DON'T NOBODY CARE!
THEY CALL US NEGRO GIRLS, CAUCASIAN GIRLS
CHINESE GIRLS TOO — THEY CALL US JEWISH
CALL US JAPANESE AND MEXICAN TOO
WE NEVER SEPARATE — WE NEVER STUDY HATE
WE NEVER STUDY WAR — WHAT FOR?
WE JUST LIVE TO DO THE SKATE — IT'S A DANCE IN 3/4 TIME
OH, BUT YOU DO IT TO A RHYTHM IN 4/4 TIME
JUST LIKE LIFE NEVER GOES TO THE RHYTHM OF CHOICE
BUT IF YOU FIND YOUR GROOVE, YOU'RE GONNA FIND YOUR VOICE
COME ON AND SKATE! — DOUBLE IT! PAULETTE PRUITT, DO THE
SKATE — TRIPLE IT! MARLA WILSON, DO THE SKATE! JOY CHILDS!
JOCELYN KENDRICKS! DEE DEE BELT!
LET'S GO AROUND THE WORLD!
VIVECA and GIRLS IN THE GYM.
MAYIM, MAYIM, MAYIM, HEY! MAYIM, MAYIM, MAYIM, HEY!
GET DOWN AND DO THE SKATE!
VIVECA.
YEAH! TINA ELLENBOGEN, DO THE SKATE — YEAH!
GO ON, BARBARA BEHMAN!
VIVECA and GIRLS IN THE GYM.
SAKURA, SAKURA YAYO I NO SORA WA, AND DO THE SKATE!
VIVECA.
YEAH! SHARON NORITAKE, DO THE SKATE — YEAH!
PEGGY HASHIMOTO!
VIVECA and GIRLS IN THE GYM.
AY AY AY AY CANTA Y NO LLORES!
PORQUE CANTANDO SE ALEGRAN
CIELITO LINDO IN THE GIRL'S GYM!

VIVECA.
YEAH! SKATE, DIANE GONZALEZ, DO THE SKATE — YEAH!
GO, SONO ARIMA!
A FUNKY LITTLE MOMENT WHEN OUR SOULS ARE PURE
ALL OF US FUNKY LITTLE GIRLS FROM LOUIS PASTEUR
I KNOW IT PROB'LY WOULDN'T WORK
BUT WHAT IF ALL THE HEADS OF STATE
COULD MAYBE GET OVER THEMSELVES
AND PUT THEIR GYM CLOTHES ON AND LEARN TO DO THE SKATE?
YEAH! SEÑOR PRESIDENTE, DO THE SKATE!
YEAH! GO, YOUR ROYAL HIGHNESS, DO THE SKATE!
YEAH! MADAME PRIME MINISTER! COME ON, MISTER SENATOR!
PUT YOUR TENNIS SHOES ON AND DO THE SKATE!
(End of song. Viveca exits the gym with Leslie, a white girl, as the bell rings. They laugh and sing.)
VIVECA and LESLIE.
PUT YOUR TENNIS SHOES ON AND DO THE SKATE!
LESLIE. *(As she exits.)* See you in English class, Bubbly!
VIVECA. *(Replying, as she spots Gregory and heads for him.)* Okay! — Hi, Gregory!
GREGORY. *(Nodding perfunctorily.)* Bubbly.
VIVECA. Hey, you wanna walk me home?
GREGORY. Not really.
VIVECA. I'll teach you how to do the skate. It's really fun, 'cause when you're skating, you don't have to worry about anything, you just — *(She skates.)* — and you're cool!
GREGORY. I don't have to — *(As he does his impression of the skate.)* — to be cool. I'm cool by nature.
VIVECA. *(All innocence.)* Really? *(Tickling him unmercifully.)* — Are you cool now, huh, huh, huh, huh? *(He begins to laugh, then to chase her and tickle her back. Nilda, a pretty black girl, enters, folds her arms, wrinkles her nose and looks Viveca up and down.)*
NILDA. What you doin', Gregory?
GREGORY. *(Jumping away from Viveca; cooler than cool, to Nilda:)* You ready to go?
NILDA. She in the class with all them white kids, right? She always trying to hang out with 'em too. I think she wanna be white. *(To Viveca.)* Don't you? *(Pause.)* You Oreo.
GREGORY. *(Bored; leaving.)* I ain't askin' you again, Nilda.
NILDA. *(Throwing over her shoulder, as she hurries after Gregory:)* You a crazy, sick, pathetic Oreo bitch, that's what you are.

STICKS AND STONES

CHORUS. *(As Viveca walks morosely home.)*
GREEN GREEN DOLLAR BILLS, WHITE, WHITE POWDER KILLS
HIGH YELLOW COAL BLACK, TAKE THE CLOCK AND TURN IT BACK
DOO RAG BLUE RED, WRAP YOUR DEATH AROUND YOUR HEAD
STICKS AND STONES CAN BREAK MY BONES, BUT COLORS GO DEEPER
OH YEAH, OH YEAH
BITCH DOG SKEEZER NERD — OH THE POWER OF THE WORD
FAG DYKE NIGGER HO — NAMES THAT STICK AND DON'T LET GO
MAJOR DRAMA IF YOU TALK ABOUT MY MAMA
STICKS AND STONES CAN BREAK MY BONES, BUT NAMES GO DEEPER
OH YEAH, OH YEAH
LITTLE DE ANDRE, CRAZY JOHN AND BOBBY J
TATA'S "PLAY" NIECE, DARRYL'S DADDY, THREE POLICE
THEY'RE ALL VERY SILENT IN THE CEMETERY
STICKS AND STONES CAN BREAK MY BONES, BUT BULLETS GO DEEPER
AND THEY'RE GONE, THEY'RE GONE, BYE, BYE, AND THEY'RE GONE
(End of song.)
VIVECA. *(In her bedroom, moping with Chitty Chatty. Suddenly, defiantly:)* What the heck is so bad about an Oreo anyway? It's a damn good cookie!
CHITTY CHATTY. Can we go out and play?
VIVECA. I'd really like to, but there're just too many black people out there that want to call you names, and too many white people out there that want to blow you up. So I think I'd better take a nap instead … *(She falls asleep on her bed; the scene changes into a forest. White sheeted nightriders head towards her; she gasps.)* Scary white monsters! *(As Harriet Tubman approaches, leading runaway slaves.)* Oh my God! Harriet Tubman!

WALK ON THE WATER

HARRIET TUBMAN. *(Glowering; pulling out a pistol, aiming it at Viveca.)*
BE FREE OR DIE, YOU OREO, YOU OREO, YOU O-REO-REO!
RUNAWAYS.
OREO!
VIVECA.
(Closing her eyes tightly; clasping her hands in prayer as Harriet Tubman, the runaways and the nightriders circle around her.)
JESUS LOVES ME, JESUS LOVES ME

VIVECA.	NIGHTRIDERS.	HARRIET and CHORUS.
JESUS LOVES ME	WOOF, WOOF, BANG BANG	YOU OREO! YOU OREO!
JESUS LOVES ME	WOOF, WOOF, BANG BANG	YOU OREO! YOU OREO!

VIVECA.
I WENT DOWN TO THE TOWN OF GALILEE
SHOW ME HOW TO WALK ON THE WATER
I SAW JESUS WALKING 'CROSS THE DEEP BLUE SEA
SHOW ME HOW TO WALK ON THE WATER
I SAID, "JESUS, TAKE ME TO THE PROMISED LAND
SHOW ME HOW TO WALK ON THE WATER"
I WANT TO WALK ON WATER, JESUS HOLD MY HAND
SHOW ME HOW TO WALK ON THE WATER
JESUS LOVES ME, THIS I KNOW …
HARRIET TUBMAN, CHORUS and NIGHTRIDERS.
JESUS LOVES YOU, THAT'S A GOOD ONE, HA HA HA HA HA HA HA HA —
(A terrible boom; a flash of white light — flickering into a dull glow.)
VIVECA. A nuclear bomb explosion! *(As it dawns on her, smugly:)* And I'm the only survivor! *(She hears moans. Larry Grimble, a handsome little thug-in-training, is unconscious in the rubble. Viveca gasps in delight.)* Larry Grimble! The boy I've had a crush on since third grade — oh, Larry, Larry, you're alive, you're alive! And you're cute! With your good hair and your caramel-colored skin and all those little scars on your face from your fights on the school playground — oh wake up, wake up and speak to me, Larry! Larry? Larry —
CHORUS.
WAKE UP, WAKE UP, LARRY GRIMBLE, IT'S YOUR LUCKY DAY!
LARRY. *(Bringing up his fists, as Viveca slaps him into consciousness.)* Hey, who's slappin' me, I'll kick yo' ass!
VIVECA. *(Nurturing, loving; gesturing happily around her.)* No, no, no, Larry — sh, sh, sh. The days of fighting are over. You've been through a nuclear holocaust! Now there's just the two of us, forever and ever.
LARRY. *(Cool about it — he's been through a lot worse in his life.)* Then you gonna be my woman for all time, help me repopulate the world with kind, gentle sensitive people, anybody mess wit' you, I'll kick they ass, now I'ma go take a piss.

VIVECA. Larry? Larry?	CHORUS.
	WAKE UP, WAKE UP, BUBBLY STANTON
	IT'S YOUR LUCKY DAY!

(The scene changes back to Viveca's bedroom. She wakes up woefully crying out "Larry!" as the yawning chorus sings:)
CHORUS.
WAKE UP, WAKE UP, BUBBLY STANTON, IT'S YOUR LUCKY DAY …
(End of song.)

VIVECA. *(Whimpering.)* Why did it have to be a dream? And what did it mean, anyway? *(Struck by a horrible thought.)* Does it mean the world will be destroyed before I become a dancing star? Oh no, no, no, that can't be what it means! But how can I know for sure? — *(Brainstorm.)* Chitty Chatty! *(Reaching for Chitty Chatty, pulling the string.)* Come on, Chitty Chatty, work with me —
CHITTY CHATTY. It's time to sing a happy song! La, la, la, la, la, la, la — *(Frustrated, Viveca throws Chitty Chatty facedown onto the floor. Sound of murmuring. Viveca looks around, confused. More murmuring. Viveca looks down at Chitty Chatty.)*
VIVECA. Chitty Chatty? What was that? Did you say something?
CHITTY CHATTY. *(Viveca gasps, as Chitty Chatty says, unaided by the string:)* Yes. I said, you'll never be the greatest dancing star in the world.
VIVECA. But why not?
CHITTY CHATTY. Because you're fucked up. Your psyche is damaged, your grip on reality is tenuous. You're very, very, very fucked up.
VIVECA. So wait a minute, wait a minute — my psyche is damaged, my grip on reality is tenuous, I'm very fu — I'm very fu — fu — *I'll never be the greatest dancing star in the world?!*
CHITTY CHATTY. Nope! … well — maybe you can be. If you go to the place where fucked-up people go to make their dreams come true. But Bubbly, that won't solve your problems.
VIVECA. What do you know about problems?! You're just an old white doll that doesn't have any problems!
CHITTY CHATTY. Oh, so you think it's easy being me, do you, Bubbly? Okay, that's it. Pull my ponytail. *(Viveca shrugs, pulls off Chitty Chatty's blond topknot revealing the doll's short black 'fro. Letting out a piteous wail of woe.)*
VIVECA. Nooooo, Chitty Chatty! Not you!
CHITTY CHATTY. I can't live the lie any longer, Bubbly. Not after watching you go through night after day of your tortured existence.
VIVECA. *(Wailing, moaning.)* Chitty Chatty is passing!
CHITTY CHATTY. What else could I do, girl? No one was gonna buy me if they knew my name was really Shateekwa Melanina Jones!
VIVECA. *(Sadly picking up, stroking the blond Chitty Chatty locks, sighing.)* Your hair … your long, straight, beautiful hair … *(Lights down on her; up on Mommy in the kitchen, behind a chair with a towel on it. A straightening comb and an old-fashioned curling iron are heating, on the stove — a blue jar of Posner's Bergamot Pressing Oil is on a kitchen counter. Mommy calls out:)*
MOMMY. Viveca, if I don't press your hair now, you're going to be late for high school!

PASS THE FLAME

BLACK WOMEN'S CHORUS.
(As Viveca sits in the kitchen chair, puts the towel on her shoulders.)
HEATED METAL COMB WILL STING HER
BUT WHAT LOVELY HAIR YOU'LL BRING HER
SO THEY'VE TAUGHT YOU, SO YOU'VE TAUGHT HER
PASS THE FLAME ON *(ssssss!)* MOTHER/DAUGHTER …
(End of song. Lights out as Mommy picks up the comb. Sitar sound. Lights up. Hippie flower children clap and snap on the "one" and "three" beats of four-beat measures. Viveca, hair freshly pressed, enters.)

WAR IS NOT GOOD

HIPPIE FLOWER CHILD 1.
WAR IS NOT GOOD FOR CHILDREN AND OTHER LIVING THINGS!
VIVECA. No, it's on the "two" and "four" beat — see? That sounds better —

VIVECA. *(Helpful; snapping, pointing out:)*	**HIPPIE FLOWER CHILD 3.**
— No, no, no, that's the "one" and the "three," that doesn't sound good —	DON'T TRUST ANYBODY OVER THIRTY! DON'T TRUST ANYBODY OVER THIRTY!

(Cosmic Rainbow, a stoned-out hippie, pulls Viveca into the dance. At first snapping on the "one" and "three" beat to impress him, then getting lost in the rhythm, she begins to improvise her own strange and beautiful dance. An angry neighbor shakes his fist, then turns his sprinklers on; as the flower children frolic in delight, Viveca exits, screaming in terror:)

HIPPIE FLOWER CHILD 4.	**ANGRY NEIGHBOR.**	**VIVECA.**
WHAT IF THEY GAVE A WAR AND NOBODY CAME! HELL NO, WE WON'T GO!	Get off my lawn, you goddamned Commie pinkos! Get off my lawn!	My hair! My mother just pressed it! Oh no!

HIPPIE FLOWER CHILDREN.
HELL NO, WE WON'T GO, HELL NO WE WON'T GO!
(End of song. Viveca reenters, tears running down her face, hair transformed into a huge Afro. Cosmic sees her. In awe:)
COSMIC. Hey, you're that chick with the magic smile — your dance was far out, man. And your *hair* — it's so — Hendrix!
VIVECA. Does that mean — you *like* it?
COSMIC. Oh yeah, you turn me on! *(Viveca beams in her "inner" thoughts. Suddenly, a horrible thought.)*
VIVECA. My mother! How's she gonna take it when I tell her — *(Mommy enters.)* Mommy, this is my boyfriend, Cosmic Rainbow.

MOMMY. *(Aghast at first, she composes herself.)* Lovely to meet you, Mr. Rainbow. Viveca, what have you done with your hair?
COSMIC. If I may interject, Mrs. Stanton?
VIVECA. Cosmic —
COSMIC. *(Putting up a reassuring hand.)* No, it's cool, babe. See — Bubbly's hair is nappy — that's the word, right, Bub? Nappy?
VIVECA. … Yeah, Cosmic.
COSMIC. Right, nappy. Okay, so like, you gotta get past that colonialist thinking of your oppressors, man! And realize that nappy, is like, beautiful, man! Like, black is beautiful, man! You gotta let that nappy freak flag fly, man, let it fly high, man, let it take you higher, higher, higher, yeah, dig it, Momma! Right on, right *on!*
MOMMY. Viveca, may I have a word with you? Alone?
COSMIC. I dig, Mrs. Stanton. Peace. *(Flower children beckon Cosmic; he kisses Viveca and exits.)*

BRAVE NEW WORLD

FLOWER CHILDREN, COSMIC and VIVECA.
YOUNG AND FANCY FREE! INTERRACIALLY
HAND IN HAND, WE BAND IN CALIFORNIA!
VIVECA.
IT'S A BRAVE NEW WORLD …
YOU KNOW THE TIMES, THEY'RE A-CHANGING!
MOMMY.
I KNOW THAT'S WHAT SOME WHITE BOY'S BEEN SINGING
NOT QUITE THE SAME TUNE THAT WHITE BOYS WERE SINGING
WHILE BLACK MEN WERE SWINGING! OL' JIM CROW IS AN EVIL FOE
STILL, THE DEVIL YOU KNOW, AT LEAST YOU KNOW HIM
VIVECA.
THOSE DAYS ARE THROUGH
THERE'S A BRAVE NEW WORLD POINT OF VIEW!
MOMMY.
I GET THE THRUST, BUT I JUST DON'T TRUST THE AIM IS TRUE
IT'S WAY TOO OVERDUE!
CHORUS.
OVERDUE OVERDUE OVERDUE OVERDUE!
MOMMY.
THE BITTER TEARS OF BITTER YEARS OF "WHITE MAKES RIGHT"
WON'T FADE OVERNIGHT!
I'M TERRIFIED THAT YOU'RE STANDING BY HIS SIDE

I PRAY EACH DAY YOU'LL SEE AT LAST THE DIE IS CAST
AND YOU DID NOT CAST IT, AND YOU WON'T GET PAST IT
'CAUSE OL' JIM CROW IS STILL THE STATUS QUO
WHETHER IT'S LEGALLY SO, OR IT'S DE FACTO, IT'S A FACT

MOMMY.	**VIVECA.**
RACIAL HATE IS STILL INTACT	MOMMY DON'T BE AFRAID!
SO I'LL BE RIGHT HERE TO BREAK	MY DECISION'S MADE!
THE FALL WHEN YOU GET HURLED	I WON'T GET HURLED

MOMMY and VIVECA.
OUT OF THAT BRAVE NEW WORLD!

(End of song. Lights out on Mommy; Viveca is now at school with Cosmic, who smokes a joint.)
VIVECA. Cosmic, there you are! Listen, I was thinking matching headbands for grad night? But I can't decide which is more formal — tie-dyed with embroidered mirrors, or macramé, which one is more your thing?
COSMIC. *Grad night,* Bub? No way would I be caught dead at that *plastic bullshit!*
VIVECA. Wait a minute! I change my hairstyle for you, defy my mother for you, snap on the wrong damn *beat* for you, but you can't take me out on the most important night of a teenager's life?! *What the hell kind of crap is that?!*
COSMIC. Whoa. Hostile vibrations.
VIVECA. *(Panicking, trying to be cheery.)* I don't know what's wrong with me, Cosmic.
COSMIC. You're turning out to be almost as much of a bummer as your friend, Emily the militant. *(He points to Emily, approaching with her pro-black stance and stylish Afro puffs.)* Y'know, ever since she discovered her black consciousness, she's been, like, a total drag.
VIVECA. She's not that bad.
COSMIC. Not to you. She'll still let *you* call her Emily. White people have to call her by her new name, Sister Kiss My Black X. I gotta get outta here, before I lose my buzz.
VIVECA. *(Slapping her forehead in a crisis of anxiety, as Cosmic exits.)* How stupid can you be? Nobody wants to see your nasty side, get it together! *(Calm once again, bubbly smile in place, philosophically:)* Oh well, I guess I'm better off going out with somebody black, anyway. It'll be good for my mother. Maybe Emily'll help me — yeah … she's in with that "in" black crowd! *(Happily giving Emily the "power fist.")* Habari gani, Emily! *(Emily, "power" fist raised, adjusts the beret wedged between her Afro puffs. Trying to sound severe and "street" despite her thick Southern California Valley girl accent, she says:)*
EMILY. My sistah, my sistah, my sis-tah! *(She and Viveca check to make sure the coast is clear. Then, giggly and schoolgirl excited, she turns into her true self, gushing:)* Okay, okay, okay, like — check it out, okay? The fascist administration, okay? They be, like, cavin' in to our righteous demands, girl? Can you dig it?!
VIVECA. Oh, Emily, does this mean we're putting a stop to institutionalized racism?!
EMILY. It's even better than that, my sistah, okay? We have, like, eliminated the dress code?!

VIVECA. *(Gasping.)* No more dress code? Emily, do you know what this means?
EMILY and VIVECA. *(Jumping around, all squeals and cheerleader-like.)* Hot pants on grad night! Power to the people, power to the people, power to the people!
VIVECA. Oh girl, we've *got* to go celebrate!
EMILY. And I know just where, girl?! Okay, Shaka Maleek Rahsaan Zimbabwe and his cousin Ricky? Okay, they be like, givin' a party tonight in the Jungle, and we be like, crashin' it? *(Ecstatically, she does a funky dance; Viveca does her own wacky psychedelic flower child dance. In disgust, Emily grabs Viveca's arm; as she drags her offstage.)* So you come with me now, 'cause it's, like, obvious you need some emergency schooling in party etiquette … *(They reenter, now outside an apartment complex, wearing platform shoes, wild earrings, and très fab hot pants outfits.)*

GIVE IT UP/BELLE OF THE BALL

EMILY.
YOU READY, VIVECA?
VIVECA. *(Nervously.)*
I THINK SO
EMILY.
LET'S GO OVER IT ONE MORE TIME
VIVECA. Okay.
LOOK BORED, DON'T SMILE, WAG MY HEAD AND
ROLL MY EYES A LOT
EMILY. Good.
AND IF HE SAYS SOMETHING STUPID?
VIVECA.
I GO —
(She sucks her teeth, rolls her eyes in disgust.)
EMILY.
AND IF HE SAYS SOMETHING NICE?
VIVECA.
I GO —
(She sucks her teeth, rolls her eyes.)
EMILY.
AND IF YOU LIKE HIM?
VIVECA.
THEN I GO —
(Long withering up-and-down look, sucks her teeth, rolls her eyes.)
EMILY. Good.
NOW, WHAT IF IT'S A SLOW SONG?

VIVECA. *(Grimacing.)*
THEN I HEAD FOR THE PUNCH BOWL
EMILY.
NO NO NO! FIRST OF ALL
THEY'VE GOT THE PUNCH SPIKED WITH AKADAMA PLUM WINE
VIVECA. Oh, right.
EMILY.
AND SECOND OF ALL, HOW'RE YOU GONNA GET A DATE FOR
GRAD NIGHT IF YOU NEVER LET A BOY GRIND ON YOU
OR LET A BOY SLOB ON YOU JUST A LITTLE BIT?
VIVECA. But Emily, why can't we just talk to these boys?
EMILY. *(Sucking her teeth, rolling her eyes.)* You want to talk at a party?
ARE YOU OUT OF YOUR MIND?!
(Apartment house party. Teenage boys with big Afros and Seventies outfits huddle near the punch bowl, psyching themselves up.)
BOYS.
GIVE IT UP! GIVE IT UP!
GIVE IT UP, GIVE UP THE BOOTY! GIVE IT UP, GIVE UP THE BOOTY!
OH BABY BABY BABY, GIVE IT UP, GIVE IT UP!
'CAUSE TONIGHT I'M GETTIN' WITCHA
BABY, YOU WON'T KNOW WHAT HITCHA,
LET ME PAINT A LITTLE PITCHA OF THE WAY I'M GONNA GITCHA
GIVE IT UP!
(Raucous laughs, high fives, bravado ad-libs.)
I'M GONNA SHOW YOU MY PECS, I'M GONNA SHOW YOU MY SEX
I'VE SPIKED THE PUNCH WITH AKADAMA
GOT A HUNCH AIN'T NO PAJAMA PARTY ATMOSPHERE
HAPPENIN' UP IN HERE! GIVE IT UP!
(More bravado ad-libs.)
DESIRE DESIRE DESIRE IN THE AIR
YOU'RE MY DESIRE SUPPLIER, YOU'RE NAPPIN' UP MY HAIR
WHEN I HEAR YOUR MOANS, MY TEENAGE HORMONES
MAKE ME FRISKY LIKE A PUP, GIVE ME A BONE, BABY
COME ON AND GIVE IT UP!
(Girls check out the boys, roll their eyes, suck their teeth and look bored. Viveca and Emily enter through the beaded curtain entrance. Viveca sees Gregory; they smile, wave at each other.)
VIVECA.
OH LOOK, THERE'S GREGORY ROBINSON! HI, GREGORY!
EMILY. *(Through her teeth, as the boys make Gregory put down his hand.)*
PUT YOUR HAND DOWN, VIVECA!

VIVECA. What?
EMILY.
PUT IT DOWN, PUT IT DOWN, PUT IT DOWN, PUT IT DOWN
PUT IT DOWN!
VIVECA.
BUT THAT'S GREG'RY ROBINSON —
EMILY.
I DON'T CARE IF IT'S SMOKEY ROBINSON!
PUT YOUR DAMN HAND DOWN!
VIVECA.
WELL DOGGONE IT, EMILY! THE MUSIC'S ON
THEY'RE STANDING THERE, WE'RE STANDING HERE
AND WE'RE ROLLING OUR EYES, AND WE'RE WAGGING OUR HEADS
AND WE'RE SUCKING OUR TEETH LIKE WE'RE SUPPOSED TO
SO WHAT IS THEIR PROBLEM?!
BOYS.
OH BABY BABY BABY, I AM SCARED, I AM SCARED!
AND MY PALMS ARE KINDA SWEATIN'
AND MY PANTS I'M ALMOST WETTIN'
AND THIS PRESSURE IS UPSETTIN'
AND THERE'S NO WAY OF FORGETTIN' I AM SCARED!
(Nervous ad-libs.)
IF I COULD KNOW IN ADVANCE THAT WHEN I ASKED HER TO DANCE
SHE WOULDN'T ACT LIKE SHE WAS NAUSEOUS
THEN I WOULDN'T BE SO CAUTIOUS WONDERIN' WHAT SHE THINKS
— REJECTION STINKS! I AM SCARED!
GIRLS.
JUST OFFER YOUR HAND, BOY — THAT'S ALL YOU HAVE TO DO
OBEY MY MENTAL COMMAND, BOY
BEFORE THE SONG IS THROUGH!
BOYS.
THE HELL WITH THINKIN' — IT'S TIME FOR DRINKIN'
LIQUID COURAGE FROM A CUP OF PARTY BREW
THEN IT'S ON YOU TO GIVE IT UP! GIRL, GIVE IT UP!
(Boys dance with girls. A boy asks Viveca to dance; she does her beautiful flower child dance. The embarrassed boy abandons her on the floor; she trudges sadly back to the wall. A slow dance starts; she heads for the punch bowl, sips and spits out the spiked punch, wrinkling her nose.)
VIVECA.
THOUGH I'M A SHADOW ON THE WALL
CHORUS.
SHE'S A SHADOW ON THE WALL — SHU-BOP!

VIVECA.	**CHORUS.**
THOUGH YOU WON'T DANCE WITH ME AT ALL	NOT AT ALL—SHU-BOP!
BEING UNPOPULAR'S OKAY WITH ME	SHOO BE DAY, SHOO BE DEE
ONE DAY I WILL BE	OOH BAY BAY, SHE WILL BE

VIVECA and CHORUS.
THE BELLE OF THE BALL!
CHORUS.
TING-A-LING, TING-A-LING, TING-A-LING, SHU-BOP!
(Daddy appears in a spotlight as the chorus "shu-bops.")

MALE FALSETTO.	**DADDY.**	**HIGH FEMALE VOICES.**
SMILE, SMILE!	"Things are not as bad as they seem…"	LITTLE WALLFLOWER, SMILE!
SMILE, SMILE!	"Things are not as bad as they seem…"	LITTLE WALLFLOWER, SMILE!

CHORUS.
SMILE, SMILE!
(End of song.)
GREGORY. How come you're not dancing, Miss Dancer?
VIVECA. Oh, I'm tired. I was just about to go find Emily and ask her to drive me home.
GREGORY. She's right in front of your face, dancing with Tyrone Price — I mean, Shaka Zimbabwe. *(Emily mouths "This is Shaka!" to Viveca, then sucks her teeth and rolls her eyes at him. Gregory says nonchalantly:)* I could take you home, you know. It's no big deal, Bubbly. I'm ready to go — you live next door —
VIVECA. *(Starting to beam, then remembering to suck her teeth, look him up and down witheringly, and roll her eyes as she leaves with him.)* Fine … where's your car?
GREGORY. What car?
VIVECA. I *know* you don't expect me to walk fifteen blocks in these shoes!
GREGORY. We ain't walkin' — we ridin' my bike.
VIVECA. What bike?
GREGORY. Ain't you got no imagination, girl? *Get on the bike!*
VIVECA. *(Playing along, sucking her teeth.)* Ohhh … *that* bike. Looks kinda rickety —

BRIGHT BLUE SKY

GREGORY. *(As Viveca climbs on the "bike," happily holding onto him.)* Then you'd better hold on tight, so you don't fall off.
MMM, I AM FEELING MIGHTY GOOD
I'M ON MY BIKE, WHEELING THROUGH MY NEIGHBORHOOD
I FEEL A SMILE BEGINNING
NOW I'M GRINNING WHILE I'M SPINNING BY
AIN'T NOTHIN' BLUE HERE, BUT A BEAUTIFUL BRIGHT BLUE SKY!

VIVECA. Gregory, please! It's the middle of the night!
GREGORY.
MMM, I AM SPEEDING ON MY BIKE
MY HEART IS LEADING ME TO THIS GIRL I LIKE
VIVECA. What girl?!
GREGORY.
I LIKE HER SO MUCH, IT'S FRIGHT'NING
MY CHEST IS TIGHT'NING, SO STRUCK BY LIGHTNING AM I
THAT GIRL'S AS "MMM!" AS A BEAUTIFUL BRIGHT BLUE SKY!
VIVECA. Well, how *nice* for you.
GREGORY.
I HAVE GOT TO HURRY TO GET THERE — I START TO RACE!
I'M PUMPIN' UP AND DOWN ON THE PEDALS
I'M IN THE OLYMPICS, IN FIRST PLACE! EYES ON THE PRIZE
I'M WINNING MEDALS! I AM GONNA WIN HER LOVE, I DECLARE!
I DO SWEAR, ALMOST THERE! I'D BETTER PREPARE
TIME TO TELL HER I'M HER GUY! HOW WILL SHE REPLY?
VIVECA. Good luck.
GREGORY.
THIS TIES MY STOMACH UP IN KNOTS, IT GIVES ME INDIGESTION
SHE CONSTANTLY INVADES MY THOUGHTS
THERE ISN'T ANY QUESTION
SHE'S JUST THIS SILLY GIRL NEXT DOOR
THIS BUBBLY, BUBBLY DANCER
BUT VIVECA STANTON'S THE ANSWER — OH YEAH!
(As Viveca turns to him, smiling.)
MMM, WHEN SHE FIN'LLY TELLS ME "YES!", I'LL BE GOING, "MMM"
AT THE SWEET SMELL OF SUCCESS — CAN'T WAIT ANY LONGER
I'M WIRED, I'M SO INSPIRED, AND FIRED WITH DESIRE TO TRY
TO SHOW MY LOVE'S AS TRUE BLUE AS A BEAUTIFUL BRIGHT BLUE

GREGORY.	**CHORUS.**
SKY!	BEAUTIFUL BRIGHT BLUE SKY!

(End of song.)

LEGACY

Gregory walks Viveca to her door; they are just about to kiss. Squealing tires, screeching brakes, slamming car doors, "squawk boxes" babbling. A policeman approaches, gun aimed at Gregory.

VIVECA. What's going on —
POLICEMAN. Move aside, miss.
GREGORY. Do what he says, Viveca, just do it!
POLICEMAN.
HANDS UP! AGAINST THE WALL! YOU'RE 'BOUT TO TAKE A FALL
FORGET YOUR INNOCENCE, BECAUSE IT'S GONE!
VIVECA. But Officer, you're making a mistake —
POLICEMAN. No, miss. No mistake. *(To Gregory:)*
YOU ARE THE ENEMY — COP TO YOUR LEGACY
COP TO A GUILTY PLEA — GIVE UP THIS CON!

POLICEMAN.	GREGORY.	VIVECA.
YOU HAVE THE RIGHT TO REMAIN SILENT	We just comin' from a party, Officer	Please. You've got the wrong
YOU HAVE THE RIGHT TO REMAIN SILENT	I'm walkin' my girl home from a	person. Gregory's not like
YOU HAVE THE RIGHT TO REMAIN SILENT	party — that's all I'm doin'	that — he comes from a good
YOU HAVE THE RIGHT TO REMAIN SILENT	We just walkin' home from the party	family — we both come from
YOU HAVE THE RIGHT TO REMAIN SILENT	It's a party over there — I'm tryin' to	good families — he was just
REMAIN SILENT! REMAIN SILENT!	tell you I didn't do nothin' — I didn't	taking me home, Officer.
REMAIN SILENT! REMAIN SILENT!	— But I —	Please leave him alone. Please.

POLICEMAN.
YOU'RE PISSED AND YOU'RE AFRAID? I'M PISSED AND UNDERPAID!
RESIST! MY DAY IS MADE — COME ON, COME ON! SPREAD 'EM!

POLICEMEN.	GREGORY.	VIVECA.
HANDS UP! YOU'D BETTER YIELD		WHAT HAS HE DONE?
THOSE WEAPONS YOU'VE CONCEALED	I AIN'T THE ONE WITH	HE'S NOT THE ONE WITH
	THE GUN!	THE GUN!

POLICEMEN.
YOU'RE ON THE BATTLEFIELD — THE LINES ARE DRAWN

POLICEMEN.	GREGORY.	VIVECA.
YOU HAVE THE RIGHT TO REMAIN SILENT	BUT I DIDN'T DO NOTHIN' —	PLEASE —
YOU HAVE THE RIGHT TO REMAIN SILENT	BUT I DIDN'T DO NOTHIN' —	PLEASE —
YOU HAVE THE RIGHT TO REMAIN SILENT	I KEEP TRYIN' TO TELL YOU	PLEASE —
YOU HAVE THE RIGHT TO REMAIN SILENT	I DIDN'T DO NOTHIN' —	PLEASE —
YOU HAVE THE RIGHT TO REMAIN SILENT	OFFICER I DIDN'T DO NOTHIN'	PLEASE —
REMAIN SILENT! REMAIN SILENT!	BUT I DIDN'T DO — I DIDN'T DO —	PLEASE —

REMAIN SILENT! REMAIN SILENT!	I DIDN'T DO NOTHIN'!	THIS IS NOT HAPPENING
HANDS UP! AGAINST THE WALL!	I WANNA RUN!	THIS IS NOT HAPPENING
YOU'RE 'BOUT TO TAKE A FALL	AIN'T NOTHING WRONG	THIS IS NOT HAPPENING
YOU'RE 'BOUT TO LOSE IT ALL	THAT I'VE DONE! DON'T	THIS IS NOT HAPPENING
YEAH BOY, IT'S GONE	TELL ME IT'S A CRIME THAT	THIS IS NOT HAPPENING
YEAH BOY, IT'S GONE	I'M TRYIN' TO WALK MY GIRL!	THIS IS NOT HAPPENING
YEAH BOY, IT'S GONE —	I'M TRYIN' TO LIVE MY LIFE!	THIS IS NOT HAPPENING

POLICEMAN'S PARTNER. *(Listening to his walkie-talkie, to policeman:)* Wait a minute — wrong one.

POLICEMAN. *(As he and the others exit.)* Be careful, son. *(End of song.)*

VIVECA. *(Running to Gregory.)* Gregory!

GREGORY. It's all right. I was scared too, but we got through it.

VIVECA. *(Distraught.)* Stupid little thugs making it hard on other black people!

GREGORY. This doesn't just happen to thugs, Viveca.

VIVECA. Well, it's never going to happen to me again!

GREGORY. How you gonna stop it? By puttin' on a phony smile and pretendin' it doesn't happen?

VIVECA. Excuse me?

GREGORY. Viveca, this is me, Gregory. You don't have to play that game.
LIVING YOUR LIFE IN A BUBBLE, FLOATING OVER TROUBLE
SMILING PLEASANTLY! ALL CAUGHT UP IN SOME FANTASY!
What are you gonna do when you can't run any more?

VIVECA. *(Bright, false smile.)* Thanks for your opinion. Really.

GREGORY. Viveca, that's a fucked-up way to be. *(As he exits.)* Call me when you're ready to be real, okay?

VIVECA.
NO MATTER WHAT YOU THINK — NO MATTER WHAT YOU SAY
I'M KEEPING IN THE PINK — I'LL SMILE THIS ALL AWAY!
I'M SO TIRED OF THE CRAP OF BEING BLACK AND BLUE
I'M SPRINGING THE TRAP, UNSTICKING THE GLUE
AND IF I'M … F-F-F-FUCKED UP! FUCKED UP!
FUCKED UP THROUGH AND THROUGH
HERE'S ONE MORE FUCKED-UP THING THAT I AM GONNA DO
I'LL BLOW THIS POPCORN STAND
I'LL FIND A LAND ALL FRESH AND NEW

WONDERLAND CHORUS. *(As they prepare Viveca for her journey:)*
COME, LITTLE DANCER! WE'RE GOING TO TAKE YOU TO A
LAND ALL FRESH AND NEW! COME, LITTLE DANCER! COME ALONG!
HURRY, HURRY, HURRY, HURRY, EV'RYONE IS WAITING FOR YOU!
LET US PREPARE YOU! WE HAVEN'T GOT A MOMENT TO SPARE!
WE'LL FIX YOUR HAIR, THEN WE'LL SHOW YOU WHERE YOU'LL

FIND A LOVELY LAND, ALL FRESH AND NEW!
WHERE NO BAD NAME OR SHAME WILL BRAND YOU
AND EV'RYONE WILL UNDERSTAND YOU
BUBBLES ARE JUST AROUND THE BEND (ALL FRESH AND NEW!)
TROUBLES ARE JUST ABOUT TO END (YOU'RE COMING TO …)
VIVECA. There it is!

WHO'S THAT BUBBLY BLACK GIRL?

CHORUS.
A PLACE WHERE FUCKED-UP FOLKS CAN MAKE THEIR DREAMS COME TRUE …
VIVECA. *(As she points to the urban wonderland of New York.)* New York City!
CHORUS.
WHO'S THAT BUBBLY BLACK GIRL?
VIVECA. Hey there, Big Apple!
CHORUS.
THERE'S NO CHIP ON HER SHOULDER, SHE'S SO WELL-ASSIMILATED
SHE'S THE PRIDE OF THE BLACK RACE!
VIVECA. You're everything I hoped you'd be, and more!
CHORUS.

WHO'S THAT BUBBLY BLACK GIRL?	**VIVECA.** Radio City Music Hall!
SHE'S LIKE GIDGET AND ANN MARIE	Throngs of hustling,
AND PATTY DUKE AND TAMMY-TELL-ME-TRUE	bustling humanity!
WITH A BLACK FACE! WHO'S THAT BUBBLY	'Scuse me, pardon me, have a nice day!
BLACK GIRL? SHE'S SO BUBBLY, SO BUB-BULLY	'Scuse me, pardon me, have a nice day!
SO BUB-BUB-BUB-BUB-BUB-BUB-BUB-BUB-	'Scuse me, pardon me, have a nice day!
BUB-BUB-BUB-BLEE! BUBBLY BLACK GIRL!	

— Get the fuck out of the way! *(End of song.)*
VIVECA. Oh yes, I've come to the right place! I think I'll get one of those cute little brownstone apartments near Bloomingdale's, work at the United Nations, like Gidget, take dance class at night and if all goes well, in about four months, I should probably be …
DANCING NEW YORKERS. Viveca Stanton, America's sweetheart, starring in her own movie musical — *Miss Thing! Miss Thing! Miss Thing!*
SECRETARY 1. Miss Thing, pick up your phone! *(Viveca wakes from her daydream in a cramped office cubicle; the dancing New Yorkers have become three annoyed secretaries who stare at her. She grabs the phone, answers it cheerily, as different bosses stack the secretaries' desks with piles of papers.)*

SECRETARIAL POOL

VIVECA. Glass Ceiling Corporation, Miss Barracuda's office. No I'm sorry, she's in a meeting with Mister Arrogant right now — ooh, could you hold a second, please? Thank you!
SECRETARIES.
I'M GETTIN' DROWNED IN THE SECRETARIAL POOL
AH OOH HOO HOO HOO HOO
AH OOH HOO HOO HOO HOO, AH OOH HOO HOO
I'M SURROUNDED BY ALL MY DAILY FRUSTRATIONS —
"TAKE A LETTER FOR ME," "COULD YOU FETCH ME COFFEE?"
"COULD YOU HAND ME THAT PEN?" "COULD YOU TYPE IT AGAIN?"
— I NEED A STOLI, A SCREW AND TWO VACATIONS!
MM-HMM … YES, I DO … MM-HMM …
I'M SINKIN' DOWN IN THE SECRETARIAL POOL
AH OOH HOO HOO HOO HOO
AH OOH HOO HOO HOO HOO, AH OOH HOO HOO —
TRYIN' TO MEET ALL MY BOSS'S EXPECTATIONS —
"CAN'T YOU CANCEL YOUR DATE?" "YES I KNOW IT IS LATE"
"BUT THIS MEMO CAN'T WAIT," "COULD YOU JUST CONCENTRATE?"
— MR. BOSS MAN, YOU CAN KISS MY ASPIRATIONS!
UH-HUH, UH-HUH, UH-HUH! MY LIFE WOULD BE SO SWEET
IF I COULD CONTROL/PRESS/ESCAPE/DELETE YOU!
MM-HMM … MM-HMM … WAY DOWN IN THE SECRETARIAL POOL
VIVECA.
OH, I JUST WANT TO BE LEFT ALONE —
SECRETARY 2.
SAY WHAT?
SECRETARY 3.
SAY WHAT?
SECRETARY 1.
SAY WHAT?
VIVECA and SECRETARIES.
SAY WHAT? OH NO MISS THING, YOU BETTER PICK UP YOUR PHONE!
YOU BETTER PICK UP YOUR PHONE!
YOU BETTER PICK UP YOUR PHONE, MISS THING!
… hmph! … LISTEN, MISTER BOSS MAN … LISTEN TO ME … YOU BETTER
MAKE MY BONUS A BIG AMOUNT —
I KNOW YOUR WIFE AND YOUR MISTRESS
AND YOUR BANK ACCOUNT!

I'M GETTIN' OUT OF THE SECRETARIAL POOL SOMEDAY
I'M MAKIN' A BIG SPLASH! ... AND WALKIN' AWAY ... *(End of song.)*

PRETTY

As the secretaries exit, ad-libbing "Bye!" "See ya tomorrow!" "Yeah, back to the old grind!" Viveca exclaims, in irritation.

VIVECA. If I have to type one more invoice, I'm gonna lose it! *(Closing her eyes, calming herself down; starting to dance.)* I can't bring that into dance class ... I've got to clear my mind ... relax ... think of something good ...
... WATCHING TV, WHO DID I SEE?
A DANCER NAMED GWEN VERDON — SHE LOOKED SO PRETTY
SHE PLAYED THIS LADY OF SIN CO-STARRING IN
A MOVIE CALLED *DAMN YANKEES*, AND IT WAS PRETTY
WHEN GWEN WAS FLYING AND SIGHING
AND FLIRTING AND SKIRTING, AND WRIGGLING AND GIGGLING
AND POUTING AND SHOUTING
"WHATEVER LOLA WANTS, LOLA GETS"
AND THEN GWEN DID TEN PIROUETTES
ACROSS THE TV, EFFORTLESSLY
I TRIED TO IMITATE HER — IT LOOKED SO PRETTY
DANCE MAKES ME FREE — FREE TO BE ME
OR SOMEONE MAKE-BELIEVE FROM SOME OTHER ERA
MY LIFE IS NEVER HUMDRUM WHEN I BECOME
THE BADDEST OF ALL DANCERS — CHITA RIVERA
THAT'S WHEN I'M UTTERLY FEARLESS AND MATCHLESS AND PEERLESS
MY STYLE AND MY MOVEMENT NEED NO MORE IMPROVEMENT,
LOOK OUT, I'M CHITA — I AM SUPERFINE
'CAUSE I KNOW HOW TO GIVE YOU LINE
YOU'RE FILLED WITH INTRIGUE, BUT OUT OF YOUR LEAGUE
'CAUSE I'M THE METAPHOR FOR THE WORLD OF "PRETTY"!
WHEN I'M ALONE, I AM LESLIE CARON
BAND.
THANK HEAVEN FOR LITTLE GIRLS!
VIVECA.
THEN CALAMITY JANE, THEN I'M SHIRLEY MacCLAINE
BAND.
WHAT A WAY TO GO!

VIVECA.
WHILE I'M IN BRIGADOON BY THE LIGHT OF THE MOON
I AM CALLED CYD CHARISSE, AND I'M STEALING A "KISSE"
FROM MY PARTNER GENE KELLY
CONTRACT AND RELEASE, I AM LIZA MINELLI!
AND THE KELLY THAT'S PAULA, AND THE JUDITH THAT'S JAMISON
THE GAME IS UNCEASING
AND THE GAME IS INCREASINGLY A MAGICAL CAPE
FOR MY ESCAPE TO DIP WITH PATRICK SWAYZE —
THAT'S TRUE ROMANCING!
I'VE GOT A WAY TO AVOID OLD SIGMUND FREUD
WHEN LIFE STARTS GETTING CRAZY — I TURN TO DANCING
YOU'LL SEE ME FLYING AND SIGHING
AND FLIRTING AND SKIRTING, AND WRIGGLING AND GIGGLING
AND POUTING AND SHOUTING
"WHATEVER VIVVIE WANTS, VIVVIE GETS"
THROUGH JAMES BROWN FUNK AND MINUETS
NOW I'VE GOT DESIGNS ON GREGORY HINES
SO IF YOU'LL PLEASE EXCUSE ME, I'LL GO BE PRETTY! *(End of song.)*
BALLET TEACHER. *(As Viveca enters, the teacher taps the floor with a cane, saying:)* Five, six, seven, eight — tendu, and fourth, pirouette, tendu, piqué, piqué, and attitude en l'air — Viveca, tuck your butt in please, this is not jazz class — jété, jété, jété, jété, and lift, lift, lift up!
KEITH. *(Another dancer, who has been watching her.)* That was good. I'm Keith.
VIVECA. I'm Viveca.
KEITH. *(Pressing her nose gently, as the class becomes a jazz class.)* You've got a great smile, Viveca. And a cute mush nose.*
MODERN DANCE TEACHER. *(Enters, highly aggravated by their camaraderie.)* Five, six, seven eight, and step and tilt and step and tilt and parallel fourth position — no, not attitude! Don't come to this Graham class if you're not serious, Viveca! And prance, prance, prance and lift those feet up!
VIVECA. How come they never yell at you, Keith?
KEITH. Because they know it would be a waste of time. I'm not a dancer, I'm just a singer who moves well.
VIVECA. *(Checking out a dancer who looks like Prince Charming.)* He's really cute.
KEITH. He's really gay.
VIVECA. How do you know?
KEITH. 'Cause I'm really gay, too.
VIVECA. *(Jaw dropped; in disappointment.)* Shoot!
KEITH. Sorry, mush nose. All the good ones are gay.

* Note: "mush" is pronounced like "push."

VIVECA. There have got to be some decent straight men in New York!
KEITH. None of them will be a better friend to you … well, maybe in some ways, they will.
JAZZ CLASS TEACHER. *(As an embarrassed Viveca shushes Keith.)* Five, six, seven, eight, and hip, and back, and walk, and walk, and turn, and turn, and give me attitude — Viveca, stick that booty out, girl — this ain't no ballet class — and step-hop, and people, lift those hooves up!
KEITH. Why don't you come with me to the *Killer Diller* audition?
VIVECA. *Killer Diller?*
KEITH. It's that Broadway musical based on the Federico Brechtweill Expressionist film *Schatzie Bang, Bang*. They're holding auditions.
VIVECA. Intriguing. But Keith, I can't go with you. I don't know anything about live theater.
KEITH. *(Stepping on her toes, pressing her nose.)* Listen, you little turkey tartare, you want to be a dancer, right? Well, this is a dance audition, so it's time to get those big feet wet. And one more thing, mush nose. This director is known to pick the most beautiful women for his shows, so doll yourself up. *(The scene changes to an audition. Dancers Sophia, Sandra, Scarlett, Delilah and Tallulah enter, warm up. Viveca, now wearing a long glamour wig, watches them, then tries to emulate their sexy movements. Director Bob and his dance captain enter.)*
TALLULAH. Hi, Director Bob.
DIRECTOR BOB. Hi, Tallulah.
SCARLETT. *(As Director Bob adjusts her dance movement.)* Thank y'all, Director Bob.
DIRECTOR BOB. Just call me Bob, honey.
DANCE CAPTAIN. *(Tired, bored, over it.)* Okay ladies, take it from the top.

DIRECTOR BOB

VIVECA AND CHORINES.
OOH, DIRECTOR BOB, DO I MAKE YOU THROB?
WILL I GET THE JOB, DIRECTOR BOB?
(They snap! snap! — sigh — snap! Snap!)
I'LL GIVE IT ALL I'VE GOT, TO GET INTO MY SPOT
YOU KNOW MY SPOT IS HOT, DIRECTOR BOB!
(They snap! snap! — sigh — snap! Snap!)
YOU'RE THE MAN WHO MAKES A WOMAN DANCE THE WAY A
WOMAN WANTS TO DANCE, DIRECTOR BOB, DIRECTOR BOB
COME ON AND CHOOSE MY —
(They pant, pant, pant, pant!)
MAKE ME PANT AND BEG, MAKE ME SHAKE A LEG

TAKE ME DOWN A PEG, DIRECTOR BOB!
BUT DON'T REJECT ME, DON'T NEGLECT ME, PLEASE INSPECT ME
OOH, DIRECT ME BOB, DIRECT ME BOB, DIRECT ME BOB
TEACH ME TO USE MY —
(They whimper, whimper, whimper, whimper!)
OOH, YOU MADE ME SOB! YOU BAD DIRECTOR BOB!
BAD, BRILLIANT, BRUTAL, DADDY DIRECTOR BOB …
(They snap! Snap! — sigh — snap! Snap!)
I WILL ALWAYS LOVE YOU, DIRECTOR BOB …
(They snap! snap! — big smooch! End of song.)
DANCE CAPTAIN. *(Wearily, for the eleven millionth time:)* First of all, let me say that you're all wonderful dancers … now, will the following ladies please stay … Sophia, Sandra, Scarlett — *(As Scarlett gasps, and clasps her hand to her heart.)* Delilah and Tallulah … *(As Tallulah makes a "damn straight you'd better pick me" face, the dance captain looks at Director Bob, who nods.)* Oh and, um … Viveca. Okay, you ladies will sing next and then we're gonna immediately ask you to read, so go get what you need.
SCARLETT. Oh y'all, Ah'm just so fired up, Ah'm so fired up, Ah'm so fired up Ah made it this fah! Oh good luck to all y'all girls — each and ev'ry one of y'all! Ah mean it, Ah really do!
VIVECA. Good luck to you, too!
SCARLETT. *(Pointing to herself.)* Scarlett!
VIVECA. *(Pointing to herself.)* Viveca!
SCARLETT. For mah song, Ah'm gonna sing "Ring Mah Honeysuckle Bell," from the show *Blossom Of The Confederacy* — it's mah Mama and Daddy's fav'rite!
VIVECA. I don't have a song … *(All gasp in abject horror, except Tallulah, who snorts in derision.)*
SOPHIA. Is there anything you like to sing?
VIVECA. Um, um — oh I know — that song that goes — CAN DO — CAN DO —
TALLULAH. *(Dryly.)* Try to remember, it's called *Fugue For Tinhorns*.
DANCE CAPTAIN. Viveca Stanton!
SCARLETT. Good luck, honey!
TALLULAH. Sing out, Louise!
VIVECA. No, it's Viveca —
DANCE CAPTAIN. Viveca!
VIVECA. I'm here, I'm here! Hi, everybody! My name is Viveca, but you can just call me Bubbly! Okay, here we go! And a-one, and a-two, and a-one-two-three —
CREATE A CHOCOLATE CAKE! CREATE A CHERRY PIE!
CREATE A STACK OF GOLDEN BISCUITS PILED UP TO THE SKY!
CAN DO — (Yeah!) CAN DO — (Whoo!)
WITH GOLD MEDAL, YOU CAN DO!
Hah! … That was the Gold Medal song, from the musical, *The Tin Horn's Fugue!*

(Curtseying.) Thank you.

DIRECTOR BOB. Bubbly. I want you to read a monologue for me. Do you know what a monologue is?

VIVECA. Oh sure, Director Bob. I have inner monologues all the time. Okey-dokey, here we go — *(She clears her throat and reads the following as if slightly miffed.)* Now I'm scrambling up some eggs for breakfast, and here comes my boyfriend Roscoe breaking down my kitchen door. "What's wrong with you, Roscoe?" I inquired. "Wrong with me?" he says. "You're the one that's been lying down with the dog-catcher!" Well, I neither cared for his tone of voice nor his bad breath all up in my face — hah! So I picked up the iron skillet from off of the stove and, well — anybody care for some eggs and brains?

DIRECTOR BOB. *(As she gives an over-the-top wink, he walks to her, saying:)* Hiya, Bubbly.

VIVECA. Hi, Director Bob. Did you like that "hah!"? I thought of that one all by myself!

DIRECTOR BOB. It was a real nice touch. You're a sweet kid, and you've got an irresistible smile. I really want you to do my show. So let's try that monologue one more time. But *this* time … *(Smiling disarmingly, wagging his finger.)* Don't go white on me, Bubbly.

VIVECA. *(Thrown for a loop, then quickly recovering.)* Oh! — No — okay, I'm sorry — I don't know what happened —

DIRECTOR BOB. Think about it for a few minutes. Take your time, okay? Good girl.

VIVECA. *(As he pats her on the shoulder and exits, her "inner thoughts" spotlight appears. She says angrily:)* Hey, Director Bob! What do you think this is, camouflage?! *(Getting control.)* Okay — don't panic — black, black, black, black, black, black … lots of black people in the South … okay … Southern accent, but not like a slave … 'cause if I do get this job, I don't want to offend the few black people that are gonna be in the audience any more than I have to … who has a Southern accent? *(Thinks hard. Suddenly, an inspirational flash.)* Foghorn Leghorn! Ah say, Ah say, Ah say — Fawg Hone Lehg Hone! Yeah, that's good, but pitch it higher! *(High Southern voice.)* Fawg Hone Lehg Hone! *(Snapping her fingers; in her own voice:)* That's *it!* I'm ready!

DIRECTOR BOB. Okay, Bubbly. Take it from the top.

VIVECA. *(Á la Foghorn Leghorn/Butterfly McQueen/Amos 'n' Andy:)* Now Ah'm scram-blin' — Ah say, Ah say, Ah say — Ah'm ska-*ram*-bull-in' up some eggs for buh-*reck*-fus', and here come — Ah say, Ah say, Ah say — here come mah boyfriend *Ros*-co, jes' a-bu-*rak*-in' down mah kitchen doah. "Whu's wrong witcha, Ros-*co*?" Ah in—*kwhy* — red. "Wrong wit' *me*?" he says — *(Pointing accusingly, as if she is Roscoe.)* "*You* da one — Ah say, Ah say, Ah say, *you* da one dass' been lyin' down wit' da *dawg*-ketch-*ah!*" Well, Ah neither cared for his tone of voice, nor his bad breff all up in mah face — hunh! So Ah picked up — Ah say, Ah say, Ah say — Ah picked up da iron skillet from off'n da stove and, *well* — uh — anybody — Ah say, Ah say, Ah say *anybody* care for some eggs and

buh-*rains*-ah?! *(Winks again, then grins expectantly into the audience.)* How was that?
DIRECTOR BOB. *(Chuckling.)* Bubbly. Call your mom and dad, and tell them you'll be getting paid for being — Bubbly. *(Viveca lets out a whoop, jumps around; she is now outside the* Lillian White *Theatre, where the* Killer Diller *marquee twinkles. Keith enters; Viveca gushes to him:)*
VIVECA. A Broadway chorine, Keith! With character shoes, Director Bob style, and most importantly — hair like the dancers on *Solid Gold!*
KEITH. Success is just a head roll away! *(Hugging her as he exits.)* Listen, I gotta go, I got a date. Congratulations, mush nose!
VIVECA. *(Sighing, she enters a bookstore, sees a romance novel. Wryly:)* I've got a date, too — A Date With Destiny! *(She hides the novel behind another book and begins to read, as Lucas, a handsome black man notices her and approaches.)* "She shivered in breathless anticipation of his powerful, masculine, manly manpower. He approached, and whispered with husky, musky, dusky sensuality … "

COME WITH ME

LUCAS.
PLEASE FORGIVE ME MY BURNING STARE
I CAN'T HELP IT — NOT WHILE YOU'RE STANDING THERE
I MUST EXTEND AN INVITATION IMPROPER AND IMPROMPTU:
YOU COME WITH ME!
VIVECA. *(Completely flustered.)* Who, me? Oh, no thank you — but thanks anyway —
LUCAS.
(As he blocks her path; kisses her hand.)
PLEASE FORGIVE MY OUTRAGEOUS STYLE
I CAN'T HELP IT — I DIG YOUR CROOKED SMILE
AND I CAN SEE THAT YOU DON'T KNOW THE NEXT MOVE
SO LET ME PROMPT YOU TO COME WITH ME!
VIVECA. Oh no, I can't do that — I mean, I just met you!
LUCAS.
YOU DON'T NEED TO STAND ON CEREMONY
DON'T NEED TO ACT POLITE, AND PHONY
DON'T NEED TO HEAR CLICHÉ BALONEY
THIS IS ALL YOU NEED TO DO:
(Drawing nearer, he breathes into her ear; she shivers.)
AH-OOH … COME WITH ME!
VIVECA. I don't mean to be rude, but why would I just go off with you?
LUCAS.
COULD BE A BIG MISTAKE — I DON'T KNOW

COULD BE A PIECE OF CAKE — I DON'T KNOW
WHY DON'T YOU GIVE YOUR HEART A BREAK
AND TAKE IT WHERE IT WILL GO?

CHORUS.	**LUCAS.**
COME WITH ME, COME WITH ME	DON'T YOU WONDER
COME WITH ME, COME WITH ME	WHAT IT WOULD BE?
COME WITH ME, COME WITH ME	DON'T YOU WONDER
COME WITH ME, COME WITH ME	WHAT IT COULD BE?

VIVECA. *(Weakly.)* I mean it's very tempting and everything, you know, but frankly —
LUCAS. *(Discovering romance novel behind her other book.)*
YOU'VE BEEN LOOKING FOR TRUE ROMANCE?
SHINING ARMOR — FULL POMP AND CIRCUMSTANCE?
(As he takes her hand, leads her away.)
FORGET THAT SHINING ARMOR, ROMANCE AND CIRCUMSTANCE,
AND POMP, TOO!
VIVECA. *(Under his spell.)* Pomp, too?
LUCAS.
AND DO COME WITH ME!
VIVECA. Well, I don't know — maybe …
LUCAS.
COME WITH ME!
VIVECA. All right, just this once …
LUCAS. *(As they exit.)*
COME WITH ME!
(End of song/reprise.)

I DON'T NEED TO FAKE

VIVECA. *(She pirouettes back onto the stage, jeté-ing in pure delight over to Lucas, who now lounges on her couch.)* Wow!
I DON'T NEED TO FAKE A TRUE ORGASM!
'CAUSE NOW I'VE BECOME SOMEONE WHO HAS 'EM!
Lucas, I've never been so happy!
LUCAS. *(Reaching for her.)* Yeah, and I know just what makes you happy …
VIVECA. No, I'm talking about the kind of happiness that comes from your heart! *(Giggling, as he nuzzles her.)* Stop, I'm serious! I feel so good, it makes me want to throw a party or something, you know? Invite a few friends, maybe my parents …
LUCAS. Sounds great, baby. Can I come?
VIVECA. You'd better come!
LUCAS. And can I bring a date?

VIVECA. *(Extricating herself from his embrace.)* … You don't see the conflict in that?

GRANNY'S ADVICE

LUCAS. *(As music rises, lights come up on Granny, shelling peas.)* Well … it's like this, Viveca … My granny gave me some real good advice on dealing with women when I was knee-high to a grasshopper. I remember it like it was yesterday … she sat at her kitchen table, shelling peas for Sunday dinner. Granny winked at me, gave my shoulder a squeeze, and, as I helped her retrieve some stray peas, she said:
GRANNY.
BOY! A WOMAN IS A MYSTERY — YOU'LL NEVER GET TO KNOW HER
CHORUS.
POP!
GRANNY.
AND YOU CAN TRUST HER JUST AS FAR AS YOU CAN THROW HER
CHORUS.
POP!
GRANNY.
SHE'LL RUN YOU RAGGED, JUST AS RAGGED AS YOU CAN BE
CHORUS.
POP!
GRANNY.
GET YOU A BACK-UP, BOY — YOU GOT TO HAVE A "PLAN B"! YOU
CHORUS.
POP! POP! POP!
GRANNY.
GOT TO HAVE SOMEONE ON THE SIDE! YOU …
CHORUS.
POP! POP! POP!
GRANNY.
GOT TO HAVE SOMEONE ON THE SIDE!
(Viveca sits, listening politely, while her "inner thoughts" rage.)
LUCAS. *(Turning to Granny.)* "But Granny," I said, in my childlike innocence, "what about finding that one special girl — you know, to settle down with, once I have sown my wild oats?" Granny winked at me, popped another pea and said:
GRANNY.
BOY …
CHORUS.
POP!

GRANNY.
YOU AND THAT ANGEL GAL WILL HONEYMOON IN CLOVER
CHORUS.
POP!
GRANNY.
AND THEN SHE'LL CLIP YOUR WINGS, AND HEAVEN WILL BE OVER
CHORUS.
POP!
GRANNY.
SO IF YOU DON'T INTEND TO SPEND YOUR LIFE IN LIMBO
CHORUS.
POP!
GRANNY.
STAY WITH YOUR BETTER HALF, BUT GET YOURSELF A BIMBO! YOU
CHORUS.
POP! POP! POP!
GRANNY.
GOT TO HAVE SOMEONE ON THE SIDE! YOU …
CHORUS.
POP! POP! POP!
GRANNY.
GOT TO HAVE SOMEONE ON THE SIDE!
GRANNY and CHORUS.
TAKE IT FROM YOUR GRANNY, BOY — WOMEN AIN'T SQUAT
YOU GOT TO HAVE SOMEONE ON THE — argggh!
VIVECA. *(She strangles Granny, then backs away in horror.)* Oh my God — what have I done?!
DADDY. Yes, Viveca, what have you done?!
VIVECA. *(Whirling around, aghast as Daddy and Mommy appear.)* Daddy! Mommy!
MOMMY. We don't kill people, Viveca. Not even in our thoughts.
VIVECA. I didn't kill her — she's … sleeping! *(Manipulating Granny's mouth into a smile, adjusting her head, lolling at an unnatural angle, into a more natural position.)* See? She's smiling — dreaming happy dreams. *(To Granny:)* Granny? Granny? I'm sorry I killed you, Granny!
CHORUS. You can't kill her, colored gal! You can't kill her, colored gal! You can't kill her, colored gal! You can't kill her, colored gal!
GRANNY. *(Waking up; jumping up.)* You caint kill me, colored gal — I'm the everlastin' kind! Granny's right on up in here — *(Tapping Lucas' skull.)* — in her lovin' baby's mind! He's gonna hear his Granny say, ev'ry night and ev'ry day— *(Grabbing a microphone; to Mommy and Daddy, as they grab two backup microphones.)* You with me, children?

DADDY. Go 'head, Granny!

MOMMY. We got your back, girl!

GRANNY.
BOY! *(With each "pop!" Granny unsnaps her outfit to reveal a rhinestone studded dress. As Mommy and Daddy do some "Pip"-style choreography, Granny works the room.)* YOU PAY ATTENTION TO YOUR EVERLOVIN' GRANNY

MOMMY and DADDY.	**CHORUS.**
WELL, WELL, WELL, WELL!	POP!

GRANNY.
HER INTUITION AND HER INSTINCTS ARE UNCANNY

MOMMY and DADDY.	**CHORUS.**
UH-HUH! UH-HUH!	POP!

GRANNY.
AND GRANNY AIN'T ABOUT TO LET NO GAL DESTROY YA

MOMMY and DADDY.	**CHORUS.**
NAW!	POP!

GRANNY.
THAT'S WHY SHE'S GOT TO FILL YOUR MIND WITH PARANOIA! YOU

MOMMY, DADDY and CHORUS.
GOT TO GOT TO GOT TO

GRANNY, MOMMY, DADDY and CHORUS.
GOT TO HAVE SOMEONE

MOMMY, DADDY and CHORUS.
ON THE SIDE!

GRANNY.
PICK UP THE PEAS, BOY! YOU …

MOMMY, DADDY and CHORUS.
GOT TO GOT TO GOT TO

GRANNY, MOMMY, DADDY and CHORUS.
GOT TO HAVE SOMEONE

MOMMY, DADDY and CHORUS.
ON THE SIDE!

GRANNY.
THAT'S HOW IT BEEZ, BOY!

GRANNY, MOMMY, DADDY and CHORUS.
TAKE IT FROM YOUR GRANNY, BOY — WOMEN AIN'T SQUAT! YOU
GOT TO HAVE SOMEONE, GOT TO HAVE SOMEONE
GOT TO HAVE SOMEONE, GOT TO HAVE SOMEONE
GOT TO HAVE SOMEONE, GOT TO HAVE SOMEONE
GOT TO HAVE SOMEONE ON THE SIDE!

LUCAS, MOMMY, DADDY and CHORUS.
THANK YOU, GRANNY!
GRANNY.
YOU'RE WELCOME!
(End of song.)
VIVECA. *(As lights go out on Granny.)* You've got to go, Lucas.
LUCAS. Baby, we can work this out.
VIVECA. I don't think so. But I do hope you find the right girl … and the right girl.
LUCAS. Stay sweet, Viveca.
VIVECA. *(After he exits, she closes the door, wails:)* Daaaaddddy!
DADDY. *(He enters, cajoling her.)* Well, look at it this way — at least he respects his elders … oh come on, it's not the end of the world.
VIVVIE, SMILE FOR ME — DON'T EVER LET THEM KNOW YOU
FEEL THE PAIN … THEIR LOSS — YOUR GAIN —
VIVECA. Daddy, smiling ain't cuttin' it, okay?! I really loved him!
DADDY. Is this the way you acted around your young man, because if it is, no wonder he's not with you any more.
VIVECA. *(Staring at him, then looking down.)* Yeah, I guess I blew it.
DADDY. *(Patting her comfortingly on the shoulder as he exits.)* Well, so what if he didn't love you, honey? Everyone else does …
VIVECA. *(Forcing herself to become bubbly.)* Yes, but only when I'm — Bubbly!
CHORUS.
SHE'S A BUBBLY BLACK GIRL!
VIVECA. Bubbly!
CHORUS.
SHE'S A BUBBLY BLACK GIRL!
VIVECA. Bubbly!
CHORUS.
SHE'S A BUBBLY BLACK GIRL! SHE'S SO BUBBLY, SO BUB-BULLY
SO BUB-BUB-BUB-BUB-BUB-BUB-BUB-BUB-BUB-BUB-BUB-BLEE!
VIVECA. *(Facing front at an audition, perkily declaring:)* Hi, everybody, my name is Viveca Stanton, but you can just call me Bubbly!
DIRECTOR BOB VOICEOVER. Hiya, Bubbly. As you know, this is for a part in my new show *That Kooky Madeleine*, based on the Proustian masterpiece *Remembrance of Things Past*.
VIVECA. And what a great part it is, Director Bob! Madeleine's sidekick!
DIRECTOR BOB VOICEOVER. I want you to improv something for me, honey — I don't care what it is — I just want to see that wonderful bubbly thing you do. So this time, no pressure — you don't even have to be black, okay? Whenever you're ready.

LISTEN!

VOICE 1. *(As Viveca stands there, too immobilized to go to the audition spotlight, we hear a chorus chanting overlapping advice.)* Smile, Vivvie! Smile, smile, smile, smile!

VOICE 2. We don't get angry, Viveca, not even in our thoughts —

VOICE 3. Just be yourself! *(Smile!)*

VOICE 4. And if he says something stupid, you go tsk! *(But smile!)*

VOICE 5. And act your age and not your color! *(And smile!)*

VOICE 6. But don't go white on me, you Oreo! *(Smile!)*

VOICE 7. Just be yourself! *(Smile!)*

VOICE 8. Doll yourself up, look beautiful! *(And smile!)*

VOICE 9. Be one of the good ones! *(And smile!)*

VOICE 10. You have the right to remain silent! *(And smile!)*

VOICE 11. Just be yourself! *(Smile!)*

CHORUS 1. *(As Viveca puts her hands over her ears, involuntarily whispering "Shhh!", the chorus creeps on.)* Sh! Sh! Sh! Sh!
LISTEN *(sh!)* … LISTEN *(sh!)* … LISTEN *(sh, sh!)* …
THAT WHISP'RING GHOST *(sh!)* … ALMOST *(sh, sh!)* MISSIN' …
(sh, sh!) … LISTEN! *(sh!)*
IT'S HUMMING *(mmm!)*, DRUMMING *(mmm!)*
THRUMMING *(mmm, mmm!)*
WITH PURE DESIRE *(mmm!)*, PURE FIRE *(mmm, mmm!)*
IT'S BE — *(mmm, mmm!)* — COMING *(mmm!)*
SECURER *(hah!)*, PURER *(hah!)*, SURER *(hah, hah!)*
SOUNDS LIKE YOUR TRUE *(hah!)* SPIRIT! *(hah, hah!)*
LISTEN! *(hah, hah!)* HEAR IT?

SINGER 1.
YOU'RE RUNNIN' OUT OF STEAM

SINGER 2.
TRYING TO CHASE THAT DREAM

SINGER 3.
YOU CAN'T MAKE A MOVE UNTIL YOU PROVE
YOU'RE WORTHY OF APPROVAL

SINGERS 1, 2 and 3.
BUT IT'S COSTING YOU REMOVAL OF YOUR SELF-ESTEEM

SINGER 4.
YOU'VE GOT TO TRY

SINGER 5.
GOT TO TRY

SINGER 6.
GOT TO TRY
SINGERS 4, 5 and 6.
TRY TO LIVE YOUR LIFE THE WAY YOU CHOOSE
SHAKE OFF THOSE CHAMELEON BLUES!
SINGER 7.
MAKE LIFE SPICY
SINGER 8.
HOT OR ICY
SINGER 9.
BUT STOP MAKIN' "NICEY, NICEY!"
SINGER 8.
ANGER IS A GIVEN, GIRL — IT ISN'T A SIN
SINGERS 7, 8 and 9.
AND, IF IT'S A GIVEN, GIRL, THEN START GIVIN' IN AT LAST
SINGER 10.
IF YOU OVERDO
SINGER 11.
HEY, YOU'RE OVERDUE!
SINGER 12.
THEY'LL GET OVER YOU
SINGERS 10, 11 and 12.
TAKE THAT OVERVIEW AND
DON'T CONCEAL WHAT YOU KNOW YOU NEED TO REVEAL
EXPRESS WHAT YOU FEEL!
VIVECA. *(Dancing expressively, she throws away her wig, declaring:)* Hello everybody! My name is Viveca Stanton. You can call me *Viveca!*
… I HAVE MADE UP MY MIND!
CHORUS 1 and CHORUS 2.
LISTEN *(sh!)* … LISTEN *(sh!)* … LISTEN *(sh, sh!)* …

CHORUS 1 and CHORUS 2.	**VIVECA.**
THAT WHISP'RING GHOST *(sh!)* …	I'VE BEEN BLIND!

CHORUS 1 and CHORUS 2.
ALMOST *(sh, sh!)* MISSIN' … *(sh, sh!)* … LISTEN! *(sh!)*
VIVECA.
CAUGHT UP IN A BIND!
CHORUS 1 and CHORUS 2.
IT'S HUMMING *(mmm!)* DRUMMING *(mmm!)* THRUMMING *(mmm, mmm!)*

CHORUS 1 and CHORUS 2.	**VIVECA.**
WITH PURE DESIRE *(mmm!)*	NOW IT'S TIME TO FACE THE
PURE FIRE *(mmm, mmm!)*	FACT I'M FLAWED, GIVE UP

IT'S BE — *(mmm, mmm!)* — COMING *(mmm!)*
SECURER *(hah!)*, SURER *(hah!)*
PURER *(hah, hah!)*
SOUNDS LIKE YOUR TRUE *(hah!)*
SPIRIT! *(hah, hah!)*
LISTEN! *(hah, hah!)* HEAR IT?
THE FRAUD, MY SWEET POLITE
FACADE, I'LL LEAVE BEHIND!
I'M THROUGH
ACCOMMODATING!
AND, OOOH!
IT'S LIBERATING

VIVECA.
TO BE THE WAY I AM! NOT TO BE A SHAM
PLEASING EV'RYONE HAS NOT BEEN FUN
OH LET ME TELL YOU, HON, YOU'VE STUCK THE FORK IN
FOR THE LAST TIME, 'CAUSE THIS TURKEY'S DONE!
BEEN WASTING TIME, WASTING TIME, WASTING TIME
THINKING THAT LIFE HAD TO BE ONE BIG HAPPY MOOD
THINK I'LL CHANGE MY ATTITUDE!

CHORUS 1 and CHORUS 2.
WELL, ALL RIGHT! ARE YOU READY?

VIVECA.
READY, STEADY! MY WILLPOWER FEELS SO HEADY!
TOSS THE DICE AND TAKE THE GAMBLE, LOSE OR WIN
BABY, I AM SHEDDING MY CHAMELEON SKIN AT LAST
HERE IS ALL OF ME, NO APOLOGY
NEW PHILOSOPHY — DON'T LIKE WHAT YOU SEE?
TOO BAD, MY DEARS, I'VE GOT NO MORE FEARS, HERE'S THE DEAL
I'M KEEPING IT REAL!
(End of song.)

DIRECTOR BOB VOICEOVER. Bubbly, Bubbly, Bubbly, what was that?
VIVECA. That was me.
DIRECTOR BOB VOICEOVER. Okay, don't get me wrong, honey, I like what you did, but it's not exactly the right tone for this show. For *this* show, I need you to give me something a little less … dark.
VIVECA. You know, for the longest time, I've been trying to do exactly that — be a little less dark. But I can't run away from who I am anymore. And I don't want to. I'm letting it all hang out, Director Bob. And if you take a good look, you'll see that standing before you is nobody's sidekick, but the kookiest damn Madeleine this world will ever experience! *(Scene changes to a dance studio; a sign says "Ms. Stanton's Harlem Dance Academy — Love The Dance In Yourself — Love Yourself In The Dance." Gregory, who is now there, says:)*
GREGORY. Then what happened?
VIVECA. Shock of all shocks, I got that job.
GREGORY. You got the lead?
VIVECA. Gregory, get real, I got the sidekick. *(As they laugh.)* I'm not knocking it

— that's how I got the money to open up this place.
GREGORY. Good for you. You sound real good, Viveca. Look real good, too.
VIVECA. So do you, Gregory. I've thought about you a lot. *(They gaze at each other. Children ready for class run onstage, checking out Viveca and Gregory, whispering and giggling; one boy keeps asking, "Is that him, is that him, is that him?" Viveca quells them all with a look.)*
GREGORY. *(Regretful.)* Well, I'd better go, I got a plane to catch.
VIVECA. Gregory — is there anything I can do to convince you to postpone your flight?
GREGORY. Well, there *was* something that we started that we never did finish.
VIVECA. *(Smiling.)* And I know just what it was. Children, let's show Mr. Robinson how to do the skate!
CHILDREN. Yeah! Let's do the skate! *(Gregory rolls his eyes, laughs, joins in the dance. As the lights go down, he and the children become silhouettes, skating around Viveca in slow motion. She sings:)*
VIVECA.
THERE WAS A GIRL, AND SHE WAS A BUBBLY BLACK GIRL
OH, SUCH A BUBBLY, BUBBLY, BUBBLY BLACK GIRL … MM-HMM …
THIS IS HER STORY … THIS IS HER STORY … THIS IS HER STORY …

End of Show

Bold new plays.
Timeless classics.
Since 1936.

THE BUBBLY BLACK GIRL SHEDS HER CHAMELEON SKIN

book, music and lyrics by Kirsten Childs

5 men, 6 women (doubling, flexible casting)

What's a black girl from sunny Southern California to do? White people are blowing up black girls in Birmingham churches. Black people are shouting "Black is beautiful" while straightening their hair and coveting light skin. Viveca Stanton's answer: Slap on a bubbly smile and be as white as you can be! In a humorous and pointed coming-of-age story spanning the sixties through the nineties, Viveca blithely sails through the confusing worlds of racism, sexism, and Broadway showbiz until she's forced to face the devastating effect self-denial has had on her life.

"…[a] sharp and tasty new musical…charming…as the show ingeniously turns professional perkiness, the lifeblood of the American musical, into a funny, poignant comment on ethnic self-denial." —**The New York Times**

"The play opens with an explosion of music…accessible and enjoyable to people of all races and genders…the bubbly mixture of humor and pathos makes for an entertaining—but not feather weight—show." —**Pioneer Press**

"Soul-baring, passionate musical… Childs' ruminations speak with wisdom and resonance not only to African-American audiences that share her experience and reference, but to any sensitive soul who ever has been on the outside, struggling to fit in." —**Star Tribune**

DRAMATISTS PLAY SERVICE, INC.